Corporate Takeovers and Productivity

Corporate Takeovers and Productivity

Frank R. Lichtenberg

The MIT Press
Cambridge, Massachusetts
London, England

This book was set in Palatino by Asco Trade Typesetting Ltd., Hong Kong,
and was printed and bound in the United States of America.

Library of Congress Cataloging-in-Publication Data

Lichtenberg, Frank R.
    Corporate takeovers and productivity / Frank R. Lichtenberg.
        p.   cm.
    Includes bibliographical references and index.
    ISBN 0-262-12164-6
    1. Labor productivity—United States.   2. Consolidation and merger
of corporations—United States.   3. Airlines—United States—Case
studies.   I. Title.
HC110.L3L53   1992
387.7'1—dc20   91-42262
                                                                         CIP

For Michelle, Andrew, and Alex

Contents

Preface

That I had the opportunity, as well as the motive, to undertake in 1987 the research described in this book is serendipitous. At that time I was an American Statistical Association/National Science Foundation Research Fellow at the U.S. Bureau of the Census outside Washington, D.C., on leave from Columbia University. I had gone to the Census Bureau to conduct research on industrial R&D and productivity using the bureau's rich but confidential micro data bases. I had not considered doing research on changes in corporate ownership (takeovers), but after spending a few months getting acquainted with the census data on manufacturing plants, I realized that it was possible to identify which plants were involved in takeovers, and therefore to carefully investigate the causes and consequences of these transactions.

My being at the Census Bureau provided me with the opportunity to study takeovers, and the motive was provided by the time—the mid-1980s, the midst of one of the largest takeover booms in history. The sharp acceleration of takeover activity was then being vigorously discussed and debated by business people, academics, policymakers, and the general public. Many studies had been made of the purely financial ramifications of changes in corporate control, in particular their effect on stock prices, but little was known about the impact of takeovers on real variables such as output, productivity, employment, R&D, and fixed investment. I collected the evidence in this book to help fill that void and to inform the debate.

Some of the chapters of this book were coauthored. Donald Siegel was the coauthor of chapters 3, 4, and 5, and Moshe Kim was the coauthor of chapter 8. I profited greatly from, and deeply appreciate, the collaboration of these individuals. I was also fortunate to have discussions with and assistance or comments from Martin Baily, Bernard Black, Dennis Carlton, Richard Day, Phoebus Dhrymes, Zvi Griliches, Bronwyn Hall, Michael

Jensen, Dale Jorgenson, Ed Mansfield, Bob McGuckin, Kevin Murphy, Richard Nelson, Same Peltzman, Michael Salinger, F. M. Scherer, Clifford Winston, Peter Zadrodzny, and several anonymous reviewers. In addition I wish to thank participants at seminars and conferences at the American Enterprise Institute, Brookings Institution, Columbia University, the Census Bureau, the University of Chicago, the Federal Trade Commission, Haifa University, Harvard University, Hebrew University, MIT, the National Bureau of Economic Research, and the University of Texas.

Slightly different versions of some chapters have been previously published in economic journals. Chapter 3 was published in *Brookings Papers on Economic Activity* 3 (1987), pp. 643–673. Part of chapter 4 was published in the *Journal of Law and Economics* 33 (1990), pp. 383–408. Chapter 5 was published in the *Journal of Financial Economics* 27 (1990). Chapter 7 is forthcoming in the *Journal of Economic Behavior and Organization*. I am grateful to the publishers and editors of these journals for permission to republish here.

I would also like to express my gratitude to the following organizations, which provided major financial and technical support for the research underlying the book: the American Statistical Association, the Brookings Institution, Columbia University Graduate School of Business, the Jerome Levy Economics Institute at Bard College, the National Bureau of Economic Research, the Securities Industry Association, the U.S. Bureau of the Census (Center for Economic Studies and Statistical Research Divisions), and the U.S. National Science Foundation.

Finally, I wish to thank the capable staff of The MIT Press, especially Dana Andrus, Moira Bucharelli, and Terry Vaughn, for their encouragement, guidance, and support in this project.

Corporate Takeovers and Productivity

1 Introduction

The 1980s was a decade of intense restructuring of American business. The average annual rate of ownership change of relatively large manufacturing plants increased from 2.3 percent during 1973–79 to 4.2 percent (an 80 percent increase) during 1979–86. In the airline industry there was only one significant merger during the years 1970–78 but four mergers during 1979–81. Throughout the economy the number of completed mergers and acquisitions increased from 926 in 1974, to 2,326 in 1981, to 4,024 in 1986, doubling about every six or seven years (see table 1.1).[1]

The size and method of financing, as well as the number, of corporate control transactions changed significantly during the 1980s. The value of assets traded in the average deal more than doubled from 1979 to 1986, so the aggregate value of assets traded increased more than fivefold. The fraction of asset transactions accounted for by leveraged buyouts grew even more dramatically during that period, from under 1 percent to over one-fourth.

These developments have led to proposals (some of which have been enacted) for legislation, at both the federal and state level, to regulate the market for corporate control. For example, in 1987 the House Ways and Means Committee considered eliminating the tax deductibility of interest on junk bonds, which are used to finance some takeovers.[2] In 1989 the Pennsylvania legislature began debating a proposed antitakeover bill (SB 1310) that would, among other things, force any active investor to disgorge all profits earned on his shareholdings if bought and sold within 36 months of a control-related event.

More generally, the surge in takeover activity has stimulated a vigorous debate among policymakers, scholars, and the public about the consequences of these transactions for the health of the U.S. economy. There is considerable evidence from the finance literature that the shareholders of companies involved in control changes gain from these transactions.

Table 1.1
Mergers and acquisitions completed, 1972–86

Year	Transactions	Percent change from previous year	Value (millions of dollars)	Percent change from previous year
1972	1,263	na	na	na
1973	1,064	−15.8	na	na
1974	926	−12.9	na	na
1975	981	6.0	na	na
1976	1,145	17.0	na	na
1977	1,209	5.6	na	na
1978	1,452	20.1	na	na
1979	1,529	5.3	34,177	na
1980	1,565	2.4	32,959	−3.6
1981	2,326	48.6	67,209	103.9
1982	2,297	−1.2	60,402	−10.1
1983	2,385	3.8	52,536	−13.0
1984	3,144	31.8	125,693	139.3
1985	3,397	8.0	144,284	14.8
1986	4,024	18.4	190,512	32.0

Source: *Mergers and Acquisitions* 21 (May–June 1987): 57.
Note: A transaction is included if it involves a U.S. company and is valued at more than $1 million. Partial acquisitions and divestments of 5 percent or more of a company's capital stock are included if payments of more than $1 million are made. Real property sales and transfers are excluded. na indicates not available.

Michael Jensen (1988) has estimated that the aggregate value of these gains to shareholders during 1977–86 was almost $400 billion. But shareholders constitute only one of a number of groups of stakeholders of companies. Bondholders, employees, customers, suppliers, and the Treasury also have financial interests in the firm. Thus the fact that shareholders are made wealthier by these transactions does not necessarily imply that the economy (or society) as a whole benefits from them. A crucial question is whether the gains to shareholders are social or merely private. In principle the gains to shareholders could be offset by losses to other stakeholders such as bondholders and employees, so the gains are merely private. An alternative hypothesis is that a change in corporate control tends to result in more efficient utilization of the resources employed by the firm. Hence it moves the firm (and society) from a point below the production possibilities (and social welfare) frontier to a point on (or closer to) the frontier, and the gains to shareholders are social gains. The appropriate extent and nature of government regulation of corporate control transactions clearly depends on the extent to which shareholder gains are social versus private.

The principal hypothesis we wish to test is that a firm's productivity tends to be higher after a change in corporate control—a merger, acquisition, or leveraged buyout—than it was before the change. Our research design for testing this hypothesis is straightforward: to measure, both before and after the takeover, the actual (ex post) productivity of the firm relative to that of other firms in the same industry and year.

Because of its simplicity and directness, we believe that this approach is preferable to the one used in many previous attempts to test this hypothesis: the event-study approach. Authors of event studies attempt to determine the effect of a takeover announcement on the firm's stock price (controlling for general stock-market conditions). Under certain (controversial) assumptions there will be a takeover premium (an increase in the stock price immediately following the announcement) if and only if the market expects the earnings of the firm to be higher after the takeover than before.[3] The key assumption is that the price of a firm's stock is equal to the present discounted value of expected future dividend payments. Malkiel (1990) refers to this as the "firm-foundation" view of stock-price determination.

Even if the firm-foundation view is correct, and the stock price is an unbiased forecast of the firm's future dividends or earnings (which presumably depend positively on its productivity), it is a forecast that is subject to error, the magnitude of which may be considerable.[4] Thus even someone who believed in the efficiency of the stock market should prefer to measure the actual (ex post) change in the firm's performance over the mere (ex ante) expectation of the change.

Moreover many people in the financial and academic communities (and this has included John Maynard Keynes and Oskar Morgenstern) reject the firm-foundation view. They subscribe to what Malkiel calls the "castle-in-the-air" view of stock-price determination. On this view an investor's willingness to pay for (hence the market price of) a security is not generally equal to the expected present value of expected future dividends. He will pay more than that if he expects to be able to sell it to someone else at a higher price. Keynes wrote, "It is not sensible to pay 25 for an investment of which you believe the prospective yield to justify a value of 30, if you also believe that the market will value it at 20 three months hence." In a similar vein Malkiel (1990, 103–104) argues that

stock prices are in a sense anchored to certain "fundamentals" but the anchor is easily pulled up and then dropped in another place. For the standards of value ... are not the fixed and immutable standards that characterize the laws of physics, but rather the more flexible and fickle relationships that are consistent with a marketplace heavily influenced by mass psychology.

Dreams of castles in the air, of getting rich quick, may therefore play an important role in determining actual stock prices.

If the castle-in-the-air view is correct, changes in stock prices associated with takeover announcements tell us little, if anything, about the change in company performance before and after a takeover. For these reasons I will not analyze stock-price movements to determine whether mergers, acquisitions, and leveraged buyouts affect the technical efficiency of firms. Instead, for the most part I will use what I believe to be the purest measure of efficiency that economists have developed: *total-factor productivity* (TFP). TFP is defined as (real) output produced per unit of (real) total input employed, where total input is an index (weighted sum) of three individual inputs (factors): labor, capital, and materials.

Differences between firms or over time in TFP are likely to be positively correlated with differences in profitability and stock prices, but productivity appears to be a more primitive or fundamental variable than the latter two. A number of economic models postulate that the rate of productivity growth is an exogenous variable that determines the equilibrium values of a set of endogenous variables including profits and/or stock prices. Baily and Schultze (1990) analyze the effects of an exogenous reduction in the rate of (labor-augmenting) productivity growth within a one-sector neoclassical growth model. They show that the decline in the productivity growth rate results in a decline in the rate of profit (equal to the marginal product of capital) both in the short run and (especially) in steady-state long-run equilibrium. Allen, Faulhaber, and MacKinlay (1989) developed a two-sector general equilibrium model that links productivity growth with capital market performance. In their model both equilibrium firm profits and the value of a stock-price index are increasing functions of the exogenous productivity growth rate. They argued that stock-price data could be used to make inferences about the rate of productivity growth in sectors, such as services, for which the latter is difficult to measure directly. But given the high noise component in stock-price movements, when direct and reliable productivity measures are available, they are preferable.

Productivity determines the values of a number of key economic variables other than profits and stock prices. In the 1950s Robert Solow (1957) demonstrated that almost all (about 90 percent) of the increase in real per capita U.S. output (the standard of living) in the long run (over the course of half a century) was attributable to efficiency growth (the remainder was due to increasing capital per worker). The economic theory of *duality* implies that given the growth in input prices, a one-percentage-point increase in productivity growth will reduce the inflation rate by one percentage point. (It also implies that the rate of real wage growth is equal to the rate of productivity growth.) Suppose that firms are producing in imperfectly competitive markets where the demand for each firm's product is a decreasing function of its price, relative to those of other firms. Firms experiencing the highest productivity growth will have the lowest increases in product price and will consequently gain market share.

Unlike Solow and other contributors to the empirical macroeconomic growth literature, who analyzed the aggregate time-series variation (increase) in TFP, we will concern ourselves with the between-firm (or plant) cross-sectional variation in TFP. We hypothesize that in a given industry in a given year, there is a nondegenerate distribution (with positive variance) of producers by TFP. We are interested in measuring the relative efficiency of each producer, that is, the deviation of his TFP from the mean value of TFP in that industry and year. To accomplish this, we will estimate, separately by industry and year, a simple production function across plants and calculate the residuals from the estimated equation. These residuals (which have zero mean) are (noisy or error-ridden) indicators of the relative efficiency levels of the corresponding plants. We will compute differences between the mean residual for plants involved in control changes (changers) and the mean residual for plants not involved in control changes (non-changers), in the years before, during, and after the control changes. This procedure will enable us to test whether control changes are associated with changes in the relative efficiency of the plants involved, and to determine the magnitude of these changes.

For at least two reasons—one statistical, the other substantive—the estimated differences between the mean productivity of changers and nonchangers may be biased toward zero. The statistical reason is that the assignment of plants into either of the two groups is subject to error; plants may be misclassified. The substantive reason is that the mere threat of potential control change (takeover), not just actual takeover, may influence productivity, and we only measure actual takeovers. Suppose that both actual and potential takeovers increase productivity (not necessarily to the same extent) and that, when some firms in an industry are taken over, the threat of takeover perceived by managers of other firms increases. Then the difference between the mean productivity increases of the two groups of firms would underestimate the true effect of actual takeovers on productivity.[5]

We will analyze the effects of control changes on the "components" of TFP—output, labor, capital, and raw materials—as well as on productivity itself. Each of these variables will, like TFP, be standardized by industry and year, so we will be comparing the behavior of units (plants or firms) involved in control changes with that of other units in the same industry and year. Under this research design differences between firms in output growth rates reflect changes in their product-market shares, an additional (to TFP) indicator of firm performance. Thus we can determine how the market shares of firms involved in takeovers changed before and after the transactions.

The impact of control changes on employees is an issue of particular concern to many observers. We will analyze the effects of control changes on both the price (wage) of labor and on the two dimensions of quantity: numbers employed and average hours worked. Moreover in some of the analysis we can distinguish among three important types of employees: production (blue-collar) workers in manufacturing establishments (plants), nonproduction (white-collar) workers in these plants, and white-collar (primarily managerial and administrative) workers in auxiliary establishments (corporate headquarters). These disaggregated data enable us to test whether takeovers have differential impacts on different skill and occupational groups.

Concern about the effect of control changes on the rate of investment is also sometimes voiced. Our data will enable us to evaluate their effect on both fixed investment—expenditures on plant and equipment—and on research and development (R&D) investment. Today's stock of physical capital is the result of a sequence of past acts of fixed investment. Similarly today's stock of knowledge capital—the ensemble of products, processes, and useful ideas—is the result of past acts of R&D investment. Knowledge capital is far less tangible and amenable to measurement than physical capital, but that does not imply that its marginal contribution to output is smaller. Indeed past research has shown that the rate of return to R&D investment is much higher than the return to fixed investment. It is therefore important to examine the effects of control changes on both types of investment.

We will analyze data from a number of sources, such as Standard & Poor's Business Information Compustat II files, but the vast majority of the econometric analysis will be based on several large Census Bureau micro-data files, the most important of which is the Longitudinal Research Database (LRD).[6] The LRD contains annual time-series data (currently for the years 1972–86) on the output, inputs, and other attributes of tens of thousands of U.S. manufacturing establishments, and it is the largest and richest available data base on manufacturing plants. The data are derived from the Annual Surveys and Censuses of Manufacturers.

The establishment records in the LRD indicate the identity of the parent firm. One therefore can (and we do in some cases) aggregate data for plants belonging to a common owner and link these aggregates to other, firm-level data (e.g., on R&D investment). However, the fact that the LRD is a plant-level data base makes it a particularly attractive tool for studying producer behavior in general, and corporate control changes in particular. The majority of firms in our sample operate in more than one industry, so one can control much better for market conditions (industry effects) with plant-level data than one can with firm-level data. Also many control changes involve only parts of companies or even parts of divisions of companies. For example, 45 percent of the major LBOs during the period 1981–86 were of parts of firms rather than entire firms. It is very difficult to assess the impact of transactions involving parts of firms using financial data at the firm or even at the line-of-business level. Another important advantage of the LRD is that establishments belonging to privately owned, as well as publicly owned, companies are included in the data base. In contrast, only publicly owned companies are required to file financial statements (10-K reports) with the Securities and Exchange Commission. LBOs, which account for a rapidly increasing share of control changes, generally involve a shift from public to private ownership. The LRD therefore provides a unique opportunity to assess the performance of a company in the aftermath of an LBO.

Outline of this Book

Chapter 2 develops the concept of relative plant productivity and explains how it can be measured using the data contained in the Census Bureau's LRD file. It describes the database and measurement issues in some detail and establishes the methodological framework to be used in subsequent chapters.

Chapter 3 investigates the relationship between productivity (and its components: output and inputs) and changes in corporate control among approximately 20,000 manufacturing plants during 1972–81. The year 1981 was the latest for which data were available when we undertook this research in late 1986. First we briefly review some of the previous theoretical and empirical literature on the topic of corporate control changes. Then we informally present a new theory of control change (plant turnover) based on the theory of labor turnover or job matching, which has testable implications concerning the relationship between productivity and control change. Finally, we present and interpret a variety of estimates of the relationship between control changes and productivity.

We show in chapter 3 that manufacturing plants involved in ownership change (changers) were significantly less efficient, immediately prior to the change than other plants in their respective industries. Their mean relative productivity on the eve of the change was -3.7 percent; this figure may be biased toward zero due to errors in measuring ownership change. The relative efficiency of changers is virtually monotonically increasing in the seven years following the change. The point estimates indicate that after seven years, over two-thirds of the productivity gap has been eliminated. Moreover we can't reject the hypothesis that the gap has been eliminated entirely, that is, that the previously inefficient changers have caught up to the rest of the industry.

The paths of output and of inputs before and after ownership change are also consistent with the notion that ownership change functions as a mechanism to "redeem" inefficient plants. The output, employment, capital stock, and materials purchases of changers tends to decline (relative to industry means) at an accelerating rate prior to ownership change, and to increase (at a decelerating rate) for several years following the change. Although the market share and employment of changers increase after the transition, they do not increase enough to completely offset the losses before the transition; some of those losses are permanent.

The sample of plants analyzed in chapter 3 included only plants that were in continuous operation throughout the period 1972–81. Plants that opened or closed during the period were excluded from the sample.[7] We used this sample because we initially believed it would be much easier to manage and analyze than the full, unbalanced panel. In retrospect we think it was a mistake to censor the data in this way, since doing so may result in selection bias if the probabilities of plant ownership change and plant closings are correlated. But it is quite plausible that censoring could bias our estimates of the effect of ownership change on productivity toward zero and strengthen our hypothesis tests. The evidence suggests that extremely inefficient plants are likely to close and that moderately inefficient plants are likely to change owners; thus ownership change and plant closing may perhaps be regarded as alternative (substitute) responses (whose probabilities are therefore correlated) to low (or declining) plant productivity. Suppose that the relative performance of 100 plants begins to deteriorate. If one of these plants is sold to a new owner better suited to manage it, its decline will be halted or even reversed. If it is not sold, it continues to decline and may eventually close. Among these 100 plants, the probability of future plant closing is higher among unsold plants than among sold plants. The estimated difference between the productivity growth of previously sold and unsold plants will be smaller if we eliminate plants that ever close from our sample than it will if we do not eliminate these plants. Of course this is not the only way in which censoring could conceivably bias our results. But in chapter 3 we argue that it is quite unlikely that the relationship we observe between productivity and changes in ownership could largely be an artifact of the exclusion of closing plants. Also the updated (through 1986) sample used in chapter 5 to analyze LBOs during the period 1981–86 was not entirely censored: Plants remained in the sample even if they closed in 1981 or later.[8] The samples used in chapters 6 and 8 are not at all censored in this respect.

The analysis in chapter 3 is based exclusively on data for manufacturing plants. But in 1982 "auxiliary establishments," which include administrative offices (headquarters), R&D labs, and other nonproduction facilities, accounted for about 7 percent of the employment and 10 percent of the payroll of manufacturing companies. An auxiliary provides services to the production (manufacturing) establishments of the same company (there were 36 thousand of them, employing a total of 2.6 million people). Due to lack of data, we failed to account for these services in the plant productivity measures we constructed in chapter 3. If the effect of control changes on employment in auxiliaries is identical to the effect in plants, then our estimates in chapter 3 of the productivity impact of control changes would not be biased. However, corporate raiders such as Carl Icahn and T. Boone Pickens claim, and there is anecdotal evidence to support this, that takeovers have a much more negative impact on managerial and administrative employees than they do on workers on the shop floor. One of the major objectives of hostile takeovers, they claim, is to halt and reverse the growth of corporate bureaucracy. Between 1947 and 1982 the number of workers employed in manufacturing companies' auxiliaries increased 325 percent, whereas the number employed in their plants increased only 20 percent. Increased centralization of administrative functions and changing technology (e.g., higher information intensity of production) are undoubtedly responsible for at least part of this difference in growth rates. But an increase in managerial slack may also be partly responsible, and this slack may be reduced or eliminated in the course of takeovers.

Chapter 4 presents estimates of the effects of control changes on employment and wages in auxiliary establishments and contrasts them with the corresponding effects in manufacturing plants. These estimates enable us to calculate the effect of takeovers on auxiliary intensity (the ratio of auxiliary to production employment or payroll). This is an interesting exercise in its own right, and it also permits us to evaluate the bias to which our earlier productivity estimates were potentially subject. In addition to examining the effect of control changes on all auxiliary personnel, we examine their effect on a small but vital subset of employees: those engaged in R&D. This chapter also provides evidence concerning the relationship between firm size and auxiliary intensity, an issue addressed by certain theories of the firm and of organization.

We show in chapter 4 that there were much sharper net relative employment reductions in auxiliaries changing owners than there were in manufacturing plants changing owners: The effect of ownership change on employment growth is about four times larger (more negative) in auxiliaries. However, we cannot reject the hypothesis that ownership change has no effect on the growth of R&D employment in auxiliaries.

We estimate that ownership change is associated, on average, with an 11 percent reduction in the ratio of auxiliary-establishment (AE) employment to production-establishment (PE) employment, or with the elimination of 7.2 AE jobs per 1,000 PE jobs. These findings are consistent with anecdotal and fragmentary evidence concerning control changes and with statements made by prominent corporate raiders and investment bankers.

When we adjust our previous estimate of ownership-change-related productivity gains to account for this reduction in overhead, our estimate increases by about 75 percent. From another perspective, overhead reduction contributes about 40 percent of the total productivity gain associated with ownership change.

Changes in ownership are also associated with a reduction (of about 4 percent) in the ratio of AE to PE wage rates. This implies that the ratio of AE to PE labor cost declines even more (by 15 percent) than the ratio of AE to PE employment. Moreover, since average wage rates of AE employees are much higher, ownership change is associated with a modest reduction in the extent of earnings inequality.

We noted above that in the 1980s the leveraged buyout became a quantitatively significant type of control change, whereas in the 1970s (the period covered in earlier chapters) the LBO was of negligible importance. Chapter 5 investigates the effect of LBOs on the productivity of manufacturing plants during the period 1981–86, using the extract of the LRD analyzed in chapters 3 and 4 updated through 1986. One might expect the productivity effect of LBOs to be different from that of other, garden-variety control changes, since both the incentives and the opportunities facing managers are different in LBO partnerships than they are in typical publicly held corporations. First, compensation of senior managers (and sometimes of other employees as well) is more strongly related to performance in LBO partnerships. Second, if the firm's earnings are insufficient to cover the interest payments on the debt incurred to finance the buyout, the managers face the risk of losing control of the firm to creditors. Third, large fixed interest obligations reduce the amount of free cash flow and can reduce the likelihood and extent of investment in so-called unproductive projects.

The LRD includes information about changes in establishment control generally but not about LBOs in particular. Hence it was necessary to link the LRD data to an external list of LBO transactions and their attributes provided to us by Morgan Stanley and Co. This list indicated whether the acquiring group included the incumbent managers of the acquired unit, so we distinguish between *management* buyouts (MBOs) and other leveraged acquisitions. To assess the effects of LBOs on R&D investment, we also linked the list of LBOs to firm-level data on R&D investment collected by the National Science Foundation (NSF)/Census Bureau survey of industrial R&D, the basis for the official government statistics on industrial R&D.

In several key respects our findings concerning LBOs during the 1981–86 period are similar to, and confirm, the previous chapters' findings concerning ownership changes during 1972–81. The most important of these is that the relative efficiency of LBO plants is significantly higher in the three years after the buyout than it was at any time before the buyout; the efficiency increase is particularly large in the case of management buyouts. We find LBOs to be associated with significant reductions in the ratio of white-collar to blue-collar employment and wages. (In this case the white-collar workers are nonproduction workers in PE, not AE employees. Data on AE employment were not available for this more recent period, so we could not adjust the LBO-related productivity gain estimates as we did in chapter 4.)

In two important respects our findings concerning the relationship between LBOs and productivity differ from those concerning the relationship between garden-variety ownership changes and productivity. First, unlike plants involved in ownership changes in general, plants involved in LBOs (and particularly MBOs) do not tend to be inefficient prior to the transaction. Indeed the estimates suggest that these plants had above-average productivity in the three years before the buyout. (Moreover the relative efficiency of MBO plants was increasing during these years.) This finding is inconsistent with the "matching" model we use to explain ownership change in general. Second, the *magnitude* of the post- versus pretransaction increase in productivity is much greater for LBOs (especially MBOs) than it is for all ownership changes. Let "before" and "after" denote the simple average of the mean productivity residuals in the three years before and after the transaction, respectively. The values of these averages and of their difference, by type of transaction, are

	All ownership changes	LBOs	MBOs
Before	−3.5	1.7	4.3
After	−2.7	3.9	10.2
Change	0.8	2.2	5.9

The increase in relative efficiency associated with LBOs is almost three times as great, and that associated with MBOs over seven times as great, as that associated with all ownership changes. This is particularly striking because LBO and MBO plants have much higher (and positive) relative efficiency to begin with, and the tendency of regression toward the mean would cause these plants to have smaller increases in productivity. Instead of merely catching up to average levels of efficiency, buyout plants advance from moderate or high levels of efficiency to very or extremely high efficiency; they become the shining stars of their respective industries.

Chapter 6 reexamines the performance of firms involved in mergers, acquisitions, and leveraged buyouts, using a new and very different data base—the Global Vantage Industrial/Commercial (GVIC) file. This data base includes information on both U.S. and foreign firms involved in corporate control changes since 1988. This file includes firm-level financial accounting data for as many as 5,448 relatively large publicly traded industrial and commercial (not just manufacturing) companies from over 30 countries. Due to the nature of the available data, the analysis in this chapter differs from that in previous chapters in two major respects. First, rather than TFP, the measure of performance that we use is profitability, or the aftertax rate of return on fixed assets, which is defined as the ratio of net income to gross tangible fixed assets. Second, the GVIC file enables us to observe firms before, *but not after*, the merger, acquisition, or leveraged buyout. Since the coverage, timing, nature of the data, and the performance measure are quite different from those used in previous chapters, we believe even this limited attempt to verify our earlier results to be worthwhile.

The empirical results for U.S. firms are quite consistent with our earlier results. American firms that merge or are acquired tend to be formerly healthy firms who have gotten sick and whose financial condition has deteriorated (perhaps at an accelerating rate) prior to the transaction. From year t-5 to t-1 their after-tax rate of return on fixed assets declines almost ten percentage points, from slightly above average to significantly below average. Since another firm is willing to acquire these assets, presumably the lapse or decline in performance is perceived by the acquiror to be, to use Albert Hirschman's term, "repairable." Mergers and acquisitions may therefore serve as "mechanisms of recuperation [that] play a most useful role in avoiding social losses as well as human hardship."[9]

Foreign mergers and acquisitions and U.S. leveraged buyouts tend not to be preceded by the declines in performance associated with U.S. mergers and acquisitions. The profitability of foreign merger and acquisition targets is not significantly below average immediately before the transaction. If the profitability of these firms has declined at all, it has declined much less than that of U.S. targets. It is not clear to us why the U.S. and foreign performance trajectories before the mergers differ in this important respect. Firm-level profitability data on post-1987 leveraged buyouts were consistent with plant-level productivity data on pre-1987 LBOs: The firms that are bought out tend to be above-average performers prior to the transaction. "Sick" firms are unlikely LBO targets.

Chapter 7 proposes and tests the hypothesis that control changes since the early 1970s increased productivity by reducing the extent of companies' industrial diversification (i.e., the number of industries in which they operated). This hypothesis is really a composite of two distinct hypotheses. The first is that diversification has a negative effect on productivity. We test this hypothesis by regressing plant TFP residuals on various measures of parent-firm industrial structure, including the number of plants owned by the parent and the number of industries in which it operates. The second hypothesis is that control changes have tended to reduce diversification. Our procedure for testing this hypothesis is necessarily less direct. Using Compustat data, we simply examine changes between January 1985 and November 1989 in the distribution of firms by number of industries in which they operated. Since the market for corporate control was so active in the 1980s, it is reasonable to maintain that control changes were responsible for much of the change in the extent of diversification.

Chapter 7 provides evidence that supports the hypothesis that one reason that the ownership changes and LBOs of the 1970s and 1980s were associated with improvements in productivity was that they contributed to a reduction in industrial diversification, the dismantling of large conglomerate firms. In the 25 years after the Second World War, the degree of diversification had increased substantially; much of this increase occurred during the conglomerate merger wave of the late 1960s, the so-called go-go years. Previous studies have indicated that diversification has a negative impact on profits and on shareholder wealth. Our estimates reveal that diversification also tends to depress productivity: The greater the number of industries in which a plant's parent firm operates, the lower is the productivity of the plant (holding constant the number of plants owned by the parent and other factors). Part of the sharp decline in U.S. productivity growth that occurred in the late 1960s and 1970s is therefore probably attributable to the conglomerate merger wave.

We demonstrate that the extent of U.S. industrial diversification declined sharply during the second half of the 1980s. Data in the Compustat SIC Files indicates that the mean number of industries per firm declined 14 percent, from 5.46 to 4.70, from January 1985 to November 1989. (The number of firms in the files increased by about 16 percent, so the total number of divisions—industries-*cum*-firms—was almost unchanged.) The proportion of companies that were highly diversified (operating in more than 20 industries) declined 37 percent, and the proportion of single-industry companies increased 54 percent during this period. Two factors contributed to these changes: Companies that emerged during this period were much less diversified than those that closed, and the remaining firms reduced the number of industries in which they conducted business.

Our data do not permit us to establish a direct relationship between changes in ownership and changes in diversification, but the active market for corporate control in the 1980s is almost surely responsible for much of the decline in diversification. We show in chapter 5 that almost half of LBOs are divisional LBOs, which would function to reduce diversification. Moreover LBOs of complete firms tend to be followed by divestitures of divisions unrelated to the firm's core lines of business, partly in order to pay down debt.

Chapter 8 examines the effect on productivity and related variables of a specific type of control transaction in a specific industry: the merger of two firms in the U.S. air transportation industry. Although there have been several studies of the effects of airline mergers on travelers' welfare, we are not aware of any evidence on their effects on operating efficiency. We develop such evidence using a data base constructed by Douglas Caves et al. (1981, 1984, 1987) that includes annual observations on all trunk and local service airlines during the years 1970–84. We estimate the effect of mergers on output price and decompose that effect into effects on unit cost and on the price-cost margin. The effect on unit cost is in turn decomposed into effects of merger on TFP and on input prices. Finally, the effect on productivity is decomposed into effects on operating characteristics (e.g., load factor) and on other (unobserved) factors.

We find that these airline mergers, like the ownership changes and buyouts in manufacturing, were associated with improvements in productivity. The point estimate of the before versus after change in relative productivity (these were defined as four-year rather than three-year intervals as before) of airlines involved in merger was four percentage points. Because we had longitudinal data for only about 30 airlines rather than thousands of manufacturing plants, the standard error of the estimated change in productivity is much higher than before, but it is still marginally significant ($t = 1.38$). The estimates also suggest that airlines involved in merger were less efficient than average prior to the merger, but the evidence here is quite weak.

Previous research has shown that the load factor (the ratio of seat-miles sold to seat-miles actually flown) is an important determinant of airline productivity. We found that carriers involved in mergers had significantly below-average load factors prior to merger and essentially average load factors after merger. Thus at least part of the merger-related productivity improvement was attributable to "catching up" to industry-average rates of capacity utilization.

As a result of their above-average productivity increases, and to a lesser extent their below-average increases in the prices of inputs (particularly labor and flight equipment), carriers involved in mergers had significantly lower increases in unit costs. Their average annual rate of unit cost growth during the five-year period centered on the merger was 1.2 percentage points lower. It appears that almost all of this cost reduction was passed on to consumers: The average annual increase in the implicit price of output (the ratio of total revenue to the index of real output) was 1.0 percentage points lower among airlines involved in mergers.

2

**The Concept of Relative
Plant Productivity and
Its Measurement Using
Census LRD Data**

Microeconomic theory postulates that the firm employs a bundle of resources or inputs, such as labor and capital, to produce output. (For simplicity, we assume that the firm produces a single product.) The general
definition of productivity is the ratio of (real) output to (real) input:

$$\varepsilon = \frac{Q}{\text{input}},$$ (1)

where ε denotes productivity and Q denotes output. The definition spe-
cifies real rather than nominal output and input because we seek to eliminate the influence of price changes when making productivity comparisons.

Because the firm employs more than one input, there are several ways of
defining productivity, corresponding to different definitions of the denominator of (1). It is possible to define partial productivity measures, based on
only a subset of the inputs employed by the firm. In fact the best-known
measure of productivity—labor productivity, output per unit of labor
input—is a partial productivity measure. Labor productivity is important
because it is closely related to, indeed almost synonymous with, per-capita
income (the "standard of living"). We are concerned, however, with measuring producer efficiency, and labor productivity is an imperfect measure
of efficiency because it fails to account for the output contributions of
other, nonlabor inputs.

A good index of efficiency must account for and give proper weight to
the services of all of the inputs employed by the firm. Total-factor productivity is such an index; it is defined as output per unit of total input, where
total input is an index (weighted sum) of the individual inputs:

$$\varepsilon_T = \frac{Q}{T(L, K)},$$ (2)

where ε_T denotes total-factor productivity, $T(\ )$ denotes total input, L denotes labor input, and K denotes capital input. Precise definitions of L and K are provided below; for the moment we define L as total hours worked and K as the real net stock of plant and equipment.

We can rearrange (2) to look like a production function in which output is the dependent variable:

$$Q = \varepsilon_T * T(L, K). \tag{3}$$

Equation (3) reveals that output produced is determined by the quantities of inputs employed and the efficiency of the producer. Choosing a functional form for $T(\ )$ is equivalent to specifying the form of the production function. We assume that $T(\ )$ is a Cobb-Douglas function, or geometrically weighted sum, of its arguments:

$$T(L, K) = L^\alpha K^\beta. \tag{4}$$

Hence the production function is

$$Q = \varepsilon_T * L^\alpha K^\beta. \tag{5}$$

Taking logarithms, we obtain

$$\ln Q = \ln \varepsilon_T + \alpha \ln L + \beta \ln K. \tag{6}$$

Equation (6) may be viewed as a local, first-order logarithmic approximation of any arbitrary production function. Although more complex (second-order) functional forms have been used in some applications, Maddala (1979, 309) has shown that, at least within "a limited class of functions ... (viz. Cobb-Douglas, generalized Leontief, homogeneous translog, and homogeneous quadratic) differences in the functional form produce negligible differences in measures of multi-factor productivity."

Our objective is to compare the productivity of manufacturing plants involved in ownership changes with that of other plants in the same industry and year, both before and after the change. Given a set of data $\{Q_i, L_i, K_i\}$, $i = 1, \ldots, N$, for a set of plants in an industry, each plant's total-factor productivity ε_{Ti} (relative to mean productivity in the industry) can under certain assumptions be inferred using equation (6). Suppose that the technical parameters α and β are invariant across plants and that TFP varies across plants but is unobservable. Under these assumptions we can rewrite (6) as follows:

$$\ln Q_i = \alpha \ln L_i + \beta \ln K_i + u_i, \tag{7}$$

where $u_i \equiv \ln \varepsilon_{Ti}$. Equation (7) looks like a regression equation in which plant i's disturbance u_i is equivalent to (the logarithm of) its productivity. If this disturbance is uncorrelated with the regressors L and K, a and b, the ordinary least-squares (OLS) estimators of α and β, respectively, are best linear unbiased estimators. Moreover the residuals of this fitted production function

$$e_i = \ln Q_i - a \ln L_i - b \ln K_i \tag{8}$$

are best linear unbiased estimators of the corresponding disturbances, the u_i.

Marschak and Andrews (1944) question the assumption that the disturbances are orthogonal to the input quantities. They note that if the producer knew the value of the productivity disturbance before choosing these quantities, the (profit-maximizing) quantities chosen would depend on the value of the disturbance, implying inconsistency of least-squares estimation. But Zellner, Kmenta, and Drèze (1966) argue that it is more reasonable to assume that the value of the disturbance is not known until after input quantities are chosen and that entrepreneurs maximize expected profit. In this case input quantities do not depend on u and least-squares estimates are unbiased.

Instead of using OLS estimates of α and β to calculate the residuals, one could use industry-average factor shares as estimates of the respective input elasticities, that is, replace α by $(1 - s_K)$ and β by s_K in equation (8), where s_K is capital's share in total cost of production. The consistency of estimates based on this procedure does not require that the disturbances be orthogonal. It does require, however, that the assumptions of competitive factor markets and constant returns be satisfied. Lichtenberg (1988) finds that OLS estimates of input elasticities are very close to respective factor shares. Hence the two procedures would yield very similar estimates of the disturbances u_i. In this book we adopt the first approach, that is, we estimate equation (7) by OLS, separately by four-digit SIC industry and year, and use the residuals as estimates of the true but unknown productivity deviations.

To estimate equation (7), we use data extracted from the Census Bureau's Longitudinal Research Database. The LRD is a large micro data base of establishment-level data constructed by pooling information from the quinquennial Census of Manufactures and the Annual Survey of Manufactures. See McGuckin and Pascoe (1988) for a detailed discussion of the LRD. Data for between 310,000 and 350,000 establishments are included for each of five census years (1963, 1967, 1972, 1977, and 1982), and for between 52,000 and 74,000 establishments in noncensus years from 1973 to 1986. In chapter 3 we analyze data for the years 1972 through 1981—the latest year for which data were available when the analysis was performed. We restrict our sample to establishments that were observed in every one of the ten years 1972–81. Thus plants that opened or closed and plants that were admitted to or deleted from the ASM sample during the period are excluded. As a result our sample contains data for 20,493 establishments.

For the analysis of LBOs in chapter 5 we extend the data for these establishments through 1986, using newly available data for 1982–86. We do not include data for plants not in our earlier file, that is, plants that opened or were admitted into the ASM sample after 1981. Since some of the establishments in our pre-1981 sample subsequently closed or ceased to be sampled by the Census Bureau, the number in our 1986 sample fell to about 14,300.

We use the data contained in the LRD to construct as closely as possible the variables included in the production function (7). Although Q denotes real output, only a nominal output variable can be constructed from the LRD data. This variable, denoted VQ, is defined as the value of shipments plus the change in the value of finished-goods and work-in-process inventories. If the product market is perfectly competitive, all plants in an industry will receive the same price for their output, and VQ_i will be proportional to Q_i. Therefore our estimates of the residuals e_i will not be affected by the substitution of the former for the latter. If the market is imperfectly competitive, however, the residuals will reflect price variation as well as efficiency variation. Suppose that markets are imperfectly competitive and that a firm's willingness to exploit its market power by raising prices is higher after an ownership change than before. In that case the pre- versus post-takeover change in the firm's residual overestimates the change in its relative efficiency.

In principle our output measure is also influenced by changes in inventory valuation accounting, and such changes might be particularly likely to occur in connection with takeovers or LBOs. But at annual frequency, inventory changes are very small in relation to the value of shipments (less than 1 percent), so we believe that any bias introduced is likely to be small.

Labor input L is defined as production-worker-equivalent man-hours, that is, as production worker man-hours times the ratio of total wages and salaries to production-worker wages. (Nonproduction worker employment and payroll, but not hours, are reported in the LRD.) This procedure assumes that the ratio of production to nonproduction wage rates is equal to the ratio of their marginal products.

Plant-level time-series estimates of the net stock of plant and equipment in constant dollars K are constructed by combining plant-level data on the book value of capital in 1972 and on nominal capital expenditures in 1973−86 with industry-level data from the Bureau of Industrial Economics' Capital Stocks Data Base. Accounting changes in asset valuation would not affect our estimates of the real capital stock.

Values of $K_{i,j,t}$, where the subscripts denote plant, industry, and year, are generated by the following algorithm. First, we computed a benchmark (1972) estimate of a plant's net stock of capital using the formula

$$K_{i,j,72} = GBV_{i,j,72} * \left(\frac{NSTKCON_{j,72}}{GSTKHIS_{j,72}} \right),$$

where $GBV_{i,j,72}$ = the gross book value of the plant's assets in 1972; $NSTKCON_{j,72}$ = the net stock, in constant dollars, of industry j's assets in 1972; and $GSTKHIS_{j,72}$ = the gross stock, in historical dollars, of industry j's assets in 1972. GBV is the only measure of assets in the LRD, but this is a gross-capital, historical-dollar measure, and we sought a net-capital, constant-dollar measure. Values of $K_{i,j,t}$ ($t = 73, \ldots, 81$) are generated by the recursive perpetual inventory formula

$$K_{i,j,t} = K_{i,j,t-1} * (1 - DEPREC_{j,t}) + \left(\frac{CAPEXP_{i,j,t}}{IDEF_{j,t}} \right),$$

where $DEPREC_{j,t}$ = an estimate of the average rate of capital depreciation in industry j in year t, computed as the ratio of replacement investment in industry j in year t to the net stock of capital in industry j at the end of year $(t - 1)$, both in constant dollars; $CAPEXP_{i,j,t}$ = capital expenditures of plant i in industry j in year t; and $IDEF_{j,t}$ = capital expenditure deflator for industry j in year t. Since values of all the necessary variables are available separately for plant and equipment, we perform this procedure separately on each category of assets. The resulting series are then added together.

For simplicity we have heretofore postulated that the production function includes only two inputs. In reality manufacturing plants make extensive use of intermediate materials; the latter account for over half of total cost, on average. We therefore now amend the production function to include materials inputs. Unfortunately, as for output, the LRD enables us to calculate only the nominal value of materials consumed VM—the cost of materials purchased minus the change in the value of materials inventories, not the real quantity of materials. As before, this is inconsequential for our purposes if markets for materials are perfectly competitive, but not if they aren't. In their case study of O. M. Scott & Sons Co., Baker and Wruck (1989) find that the company sought, and was able to obtain, more favorable terms from suppliers (equivalent to a reduction in materials prices) after the firm was bought out than before. If this is true of LBOs generally, then pre- versus postbuyout changes in residuals will overstate pure efficiency increases.

The modifications to equation (7) described above result in the following equation:

$$\ln VQ_i = \alpha \ln L_i + \beta \ln K_i + \delta \ln VM_i + u_i. \tag{9}$$

The regressors of (9) represent inputs employed in plant i. Some of the inputs that contribute to the plant's output, however, may not be employed in the plant itself. They may be used in nonproduction facilities, such as corporate headquarters and R&D labs, that have no shipments but provide services to manufacturing plants. In 1982 these auxiliary establishments accounted for about 7 percent of employment and 10 percent of payroll in the U.S. manufacturing sector. In chapter 4 we analyze data from censuses of auxiliaries for the years 1977 and 1982 (the data are collected quinquenially) in order to correct biases in the productivity estimates of chapter 3, which were based entirely on manufacturing establishment data. But because data from the 1987 census were not yet available, we could not perform the corresponding correction to chapter 6's productivity estimates for plants involved in LBOs during 1981–86. Failure to account for auxiliary inputs will bias our estimate of the effect of LBOs on plant productivity only if LBOs tend to alter the ratio R of auxiliary-establishment to production-establishment inputs (e.g., employment). Jensen (1989, 3) and Kravis (1989, 71) provide anecdotal evidence that LBOs tend to reduce this ratio, and chapter 4 presents econometric evidence consistent with the hypothesis that ownership changes in general reduce it.[1] If so, our estimate of the effect of LBOs on productivity will be biased downward.

We estimate equation (9) by OLS separately by industry and year and compute the residuals from these regressions. Subject to the assumptions and qualifications discussed above, each residual is an estimate of the deviation of the plant's productivity from mean productivity in that industry and year.

Total-Factor Productivity Growth

In chapter 3 we will analyze *growth rates* as well as *levels* of the productivity of plants. One way to calculate plant i's relative (to industry mean) productivity growth between year t and $t + i$ is to subtract its estimated residual from equation (9) in year t from its residual in year $t + i$. We will instead follow the more conventional, "index number" approach to measuring productivity growth as the growth rate of output minus the growth rate of a Tornqvist index of inputs:

$$\ln\left(\frac{\text{TFP}_{t+i}}{\text{TFP}_t}\right) = \ln\left(\frac{Q_{t+i}}{Q_t}\right)$$

$$- [0.5 * (S_{L,t+i} + S_{L,t})] \ln\left(\frac{L_{t+i}}{L_t}\right)$$

$$- [0.5 * (S_{K,t+i} + S_{K,t})] \ln\left(\frac{K_{t+i}}{K_t}\right)$$

$$- [0.5 * (S_{M,t+i} + S_{M,t})] \ln\left(\frac{M_{t+i}}{M_t}\right),$$

where S_L, S_K, and S_M are the shares of labor, capital, and materials, respectively, in total cost. In addition to L and K, the construction of which we described above, this approach requires estimates of real values of output Q, materials (including energy) M, and factor shares. The LRD file provides data on nominal values of shipments VQ, materials VM, and changes in inventories. The construction of real Q and M requires deflators. These deflators were imported from two separate files: (1) the Bureau of Industrial Economics Output data base, which contains deflators for raw materials, work in process, finished-goods inventories, and shipments at the four-digit SIC level for 1972–80 and (2) the National Bureau of Economic Research R&D and productivity project file, which provides materials and energy deflators at the four-digit SIC level.

Output in current dollars is defined as the value of shipments TVS, with adjustments for the net annual change in finished goods FGI, and work-in-process inventories WIPI:

$$VQ = \text{TVS} + (\text{endFGI} - \text{begFGI}) + (\text{endWIPI} - \text{begWIPI}),$$

where a V appearing before Q, K, L, or M refers to a nominal value. Real output is computed by dividing each term on the right-hand side of the equation by its corresponding industry price deflator D:

$$Q = DTVS + (DendFGI - DbegFGI) + (DendWIPI - DbegWIPI).$$

Current dollar values of materials, including energy, are defined as cost of materials taken from the LRD file plus an adjustment for the net change in materials inventories: $VM = CM - (\text{endMATI} - \text{begMATI})$. Constant dollar values of materials were evaluated by dividing current dollar values by the NBER four-digit SIC price deflators for materials and energy: $M = VM/PM$. We also computed factor shares, which were used in constructing TFP:

$$S_M = \frac{VM}{VQ},$$

$$S_L = \frac{VL}{VQ},$$

$$S_K = 1 - S_M - S_L.$$

Productivity and Changes in Ownership of Manufacturing Plants

with Donald Siegel

Various studies have attempted to determine the effect of mergers and acquisitions on efficiency, and most have used data at the level of the individual firm to examine the effects on such variables as stock prices, profits, and market share.[1] The approach taken in this chapter differs in two important respects: the level of aggregation of the data and our metric of efficiency. We investigate the determinants and effects of ownership change at the level of the individual plant by examining the behavior of total factor productivity. This research design offers two significant advantages. First, the data allow us to examine the effects of certain transactions that have not been observed before. Since many ownership changes involve only parts of companies or even parts of divisions of companies, it is very difficult to assess the impact of such partial acquisitions and divestitures using financial data at the level of the company or even of the line of business. Second, there is a consensus that the best way to measure the efficiency of an enterprise (or of an economic system) is to measure its total factor productivity.

This chapter analyzes the relationship between total-factor productivity and ownership change, using Census Bureau data on more than 18,000 relatively large plants throughout the U.S. manufacturing sector. About 21 percent of the plants changed owners at least once during a ten-year period. The data enable us to compare, both before and after ownership change, the productivity of these plants with that of plants in the same industry that have not changed owners.

This methodology allows us to address an important issue in the debate about the market for corporate control: Do the gains that typically accrue to shareholders from changes in ownership benefit society as a whole or are they merely private gains? A large body of empirical evidence on the combined market values of acquiring and acquired companies suggests that takeovers have a positive net effect on stockholder wealth. But are these private or social gains? Andrei Shleifer and Lawrence H. Summers (1988) argue that takeovers may harm those who have a stake in a company's performance—workers, suppliers, the government, the surrounding community—through layoffs, lower wages, abrogated contracts with suppliers, and lost tax revenues. They contend that increases in stock prices associated with mergers merely reflect a transfer of wealth from a firm's stakeholders to its shareholders. An opposing view is that acquisitions yield social gains because plants are then operated more efficiently. An analysis of the relationship between takeovers and total factor productivity allows the validity of these two views to be considered and compared.

Theories of Ownership Change

Many theories of ownership change have been proposed, each with different implications for how mergers and acquisitions affect economic performance. In the neoclassical tradition Meade (1968) argues that corporate takeovers promote economic natural selection. Efficient firms survive (i.e., they remain autonomous), while inefficient companies are taken over. The threat of takeover causes managers to try to maximize profits. Manne (1965) contended that the threat of takeover is serious because ownership change provides a way of getting rid of ineffective managers. In a similar vein Jensen (1988) asserted that mergers increase the efficiency of resource allocation and provide a framework for ensuring that management will act to maximize shareholder wealth.

In contrast to the neoclassical arguement, Mueller (1969) contended that corporate leaders pursue a policy of growth rather than maximization of profit or stockholder wealth.[2] Executive compensation is often based on revenue increases, and because of imperfections in capital markets, large firms are less likely to be taken over. Consistent with this notion of management empire building, Roll (1986) argued that the net effect of mergers is to reduce stockholder wealth because acquiring firms systematically overestimate the value of their targets. He attributed this myopic behavior to the hubris of top-level executives.

Gort's (1969) theory of economic disturbance implied that mergers have a neutral effect on efficiency. His model treated assets transferred through ownership change in the same manner as other income-producing assets. Mergers, he argues, are caused mainly by divergent expectations: the acquiring and acquired firms have vastly different perceptions of the present value of the target company's stock based on different expectations about future levels and sources of income. These discrepancies, he added, are more likely to occur during periods of economic disturbance—bull markets or rapid technological change.[3]

These theories of course do not constitute a complete summary of merger motives. Other reasons for takeovers frequently cited include the drive for monopoly power and the desire to achieve tax savings (see Auerbach and Reishus (1988)).

A "Matching" Theory of Ownership Change

We believe ownership change is primarily a mechanism for correcting lapses of efficiency. Most acquisitions are precipitated by a deterioration in the target firm's economic performance. Deteriorating productivity provides an important signal to a plant's owner that for some reason he is operating in a less efficient manner than an alternative parent could. This may be due to an inherent incompatibility between plant and owner (a comparative disadvantage) or an overall lack of managerial competence (an absolute disadvantage).

To account for the sources of incompatibility between plant and parent company, we note the similarity between their relationship and the one between workers and employers. In the job separation model advanced by Jovanovic (1979), the employee's true productivity in a given firm is unknown before he or she is hired. The employer's knowledge of the worker's ability improves as job tenure increases. Heterogeneous groups of workers and employers thus continually engage in a matching process, and experience provides important new information concerning the quality of the match.[4]

We believe that the theory of ownership change or plant turnover is closely related to the matching theory of job turnover. Before acquiring or building a plant, corporations (especially highly diversified ones) have incomplete information about the true levels of efficiency of these heterogeneous plants. The companies are interested only in maintaining control of establishments they can manage effectively. In this sense firms are constantly evaluating the match or fit between plant and parent. More precise information about the quality of the match develops the longer a firm operates a plant.

The matching theory of plant turnover entails three primary assumptions: (1) Some owners enjoy a comparative advantage with respect to certain plants. The source of a firm's comparative advantage may be a combination of its managerial expertise, technological skill, and ability to exploit opportunities for economies of scale or scope. (2) The quality of the match is the major determinant of the corporate-level decision to maintain or relinquish ownership of an establishment. In this regard we need not assume that there are good owners and bad owners or plants but only that there are good and bad matches.[5] (3) The quality of the match is indexed by total-factor productivity, our measure of efficiency, which is a good whose quality is determined by experience. Owners cannot determine the efficiency of plants in advance. The nature of their comparative advantage becomes evident only as they operate the facilities.

The following illustration describes the matching process. Plants and their owners are matched initially at time 0. Match quality, and hence productivity, varies randomly. The lower the plant productivity is, relative to the mean level of efficiency in the industry, the higher the probability of ownership change. Because of transactions costs associated with selling a plant, there is a threshold below which the relative efficiency of the plant must fall before a change in ownership is sensible. When an ownership change does occur, even an average match leads to above-average growth in productivity or an increase in efficiency.

The matching theory of plant turnover has two major implications: (1) A low level of productivity, which indicates a poor match, will induce a change in ownership, and (2) a change in ownership will result in an increase in productivity. The quality of each match, which is measured by the level of plant productivity, is assumed to be randomly distributed.[6] Thus the expected value of a new match (from an identical distribution) is higher, given that the first match was low.

Data

In chapter 2 we described how the data contained in the Longitudinal Research Data (LRD) file and other files were used to measure both the level and growth rate of a plant's relative productivity. We analyze in this chapter a "balanced" extract of the full LRD file, called the LRD time-series file. In this data set 20,493 manufacturing plants owned by more than 5,700 firms were observed annually from 1972 to 1981. A Census Bureau coverage code was provided in all years, allowing changes in corporate ownership to be identified. Each plant was also assigned a four-digit standard industrial classification (SIC) code based on its primary product and a code

Table 3.1
Employment and value of shipments for LRD sample plants and for total manufacturing sector, 1977

Item	Total Sample	Population	Percent
Employment (thousands)	10,275	18,515	55.5
Plants (thousands)	20.5	350.7	5.9
Shipments (billions of dollars)	909	1,359	66.9
Shipments per plant	44.4	3.9	—
Employment per plant	501.4	52.8	—

Source: Population values are derived from the U.S. Bureau of the Census, *1977 Census of Manufactures, Subject Statistics*, vol. 1 (Washington: Government Printing Office, 1981), p. 1.7.

identifying the ultimate corporate owner. Table 3.1 shows the LRD time-series sample and the total manufacturing sector population employment, plants, and values of shipments. The sample plants account for 67 percent of the total value of manufacturing shipments and 55 percent of employment. Among two-digit SICs (not shown), the industries with the highest percentages of plants included in the sample are primary metals, petroleum, tobacco, textiles, paper, and chemicals.

From both cross-sectional and time-series perspectives, the ownership changes recorded in the data set constitute a nonrandom sample of all postwar ownership changes. The LRD time-series file contains data only for continuously operating plants that were included in the Annual Survey of Manufactures (ASM) sample throughout the 1972–81 period. The 1977 Census of Manufactures (basically, the complete population of manufacturing plants) included 350,648 plants, and the LRD time-series file 20,493. The difference between the LRD file and its time-series extract is due to plant failures and changes in the ASM sample, which was redrawn in 1974 and again in 1979. The unique cross-sectional and time-series aspects of these establishments with respect to the population of manufacturing plants will be examined in detail below. Given the nonrandom distribution of the plants we observed, the ownership changes involving them are nonrepresentative. This issue will also be addressed.

The cross section in the sample consists mainly of large plants, which is not surprising because the LRD documentation explains that large plants owned by larger-than-average firms are disproportionately represented in the file. Table 3.1 shows that LRD time-series plants, although comparatively few, are 10 or 12 times as large in terms of employment and output, respectively, as the typical manufacturing plant. Approximately 82 percent of the time-series plants employed at least 250 workers, 28.8 percent employed between 250 and 499, and 52.7 had more than 500. The corresponding figures for the population of manufacturing plants were 4 percent with at least 250 workers, 2.5 percent with 250 to 499 workers, and 1.7 percent with more than 500.

Another special characteristic of the time-series file is that only establishments in continuous operation are observed; plants that close or fail are not included. In addition to selling a plant or continuing to operate it, the owner may of course choose to shut it down. Owners of the plants in the time-series file have not adopted this option. Therefore transactions involving these establishments are all successful in the sense that changes in ownership did not lead to plant closings.

Plant failures are common among U.S. manufacturing plants. Dunne, Roberts, and Samuelson (1987) have reported a failure rate between two consecutive quinquennial Censuses of Manufactures of 30 percent for the population of manufacturing plants; 56 percent of all plants sampled in 1972 had ceased operations by 1982. However, they emphasized that failure rates are sharply lower for larger, older establishments—exactly those that dominate the time-series file. They calculated a failure rate of only 10 percent for plants with more than 250 employees (82 percent of our sample) that are at least 20 years old. Unfortunately, population estimates of the percentage of plants that changed owners before closure are unavailable. Thus we are unable to determine whether new owners are especially likely to close plants.

Plant openings are also excluded from the sample. Openings perform an important function in the evolution of many industries. Dunne and Roberts (1986) have reported that approximately 150,000 plants were born between 1972 and 1977 and another 137,000 by 1982. Because of the structure of the Time Series file, we did not observe ownership changes of these fledgling plants.

The ownership changes in this sample may also be nonrepresentative from a time-series perspective. Merger activity increased substantially in the 1960s, peaking near the end of the decade; conglomerate mergers were especially popular. Based on data from W. T. Grimm (1987), Ravenscraft and Scherer estimated that 40 percent of corporate acquisitions in the 1970s were spin-offs of previously acquired units. Using the Federal Trade Commission's line-of-business data, they found that 70 percent of all lines of business that were completely sold off from 1974 to 1981 had originally been purchased by their parent companies. Given the proximity of the time frame of our sample to the wave of conglomerate mergers in the 1960s, it is likely that the ownership changes we observed reflect an unusually high percentage of spin-offs of units acquired through conglomerate mergers.

Ownership Change

Plant ownership change is a key variable in our analysis. Each plant is assigned a two-digit coverage code that identifies establishments that have experienced a change in operational status from the previous year. Several values of the coverage code relate specifically to plant acquisitions by an ultimate parent. For example, if company A owns a division with several plants and sells it to company B, we assigned each plant in the division an acquisition-related coverage code after the deal was consummated. Sales of individual plants in a division led to acquisition-related coverage codes only for those that were actually sold.

Each establishment was also assigned an identification number containing a unique six-digit code for its parent company. In principle these codes could be used to identify new owners (ultimate parents). However, changes in plant identification numbers are a potentially misleading indicator of ownership change. According to Dunne and Roberts (1986) and the LRD documentation, plant identification numbers were improperly assigned in 1972 and 1978. Furthermore the numbers can change for reasons unrelated to mergers and acquisitions, such as legal reorganization or other changes in organizational status.[7] Therefore we defined changes in ownership solely on the basis of coverage codes.

From 1972 to 1981 nearly 21 percent of the 20,500 plants in the sample experienced at least one ownership change, a turnover rate that showed remarkably little variation across two-digit SICs. Except for tobacco and miscellaneous manufacturing establishments, the percentage of plants changing owners ranged only from 14.9 to 23.8 percent. When ownership

Table 3.2
Annual changes in ownership for 20,493 manufacturing plants (unweighted), 1972–81

Year	Plants changing owners (percent)	Year	Plants changing owners (percent)
1972	3.0	1977	1.7
1973	0.9[a]	1978	2.2
1974	3.2	1979	2.4
1975	2.7	1980	3.3
1976	1.6	1981	4.1

Source: Derived from LRD sample.
a. Coverage codes apparently were not properly assigned to plants in 1973: According to data from W. T. Grimm and Co., *Mergerstat Review*, 1985 (Chicago: Grimm, 1986), 1973 was a year of moderate sell-off activity. Therefore our analysis does not include ownership changes occurring in 1973.

changes were weighted by plant employment, a proxy for plant size, the average turnover rate was 15 percent, signifying that smaller establishments are more likely to be acquired and sold. Table 3.2 shows the unweighted annual percentages of plant turnovers and indicates that, except for 1973, acquisition activity among these large plants essentially mirrored the patterns of aggregate merger activity shown in table 1.1. Unforunately, data on the incidence of ownership change among the total population of manufacturing plants are unavailable. Also we are unable to distinguish between different "types" of ownership change, such as between friendly and hostile takeovers.

Empirical Results

One important implication of the model just outlined is that plants with low productivity due to a poor match are more likely to change owners than those with good matches. To test this hypothesis, we estimated a probit regression model, OC7480 = f(RELTFP73, EMP73), where OC7480 is a dummy variable denoting whether a plant changed owners at least once from 1974 to 1980, RELTFP73 is a plant's 1973 level of productivity normalized by industry, and EMP73 is the log of a plant's 1973 level of employment normalized by industry. The estimates of the probit equation presented below (t-statistics in parentheses) were consistent with this hypothesis. There was a highly significant inverse relationship between initial productivity and subsequent plant turnover.

Initial productivity (residual)	Log plant employment, 1973	Constant	Log likelihood ratio
−0.321	−0.066	−1.111	69.98
(6.49)	(5.15)	(95.75)	—

In principle other variables, such as unionization or the extent of certain types of fixed investment, can influence the ownership change, so it is desirable to include additional covariates. Ravenscraft and Scherer (1987) considered many possible determinants of divisional (line-of-business) divestiture, including profitability of the firm, strategic variables (line-of-business market share, research and development costs, and advertising costs), and various dummy variables relating to previous merger activity within each line of business. Such explanatory variables are excluded from our ownership change equation because they were unobserved or because

Table 3.3
Relationship between manufacturing plant productivity in 1973 and ownership change in 1974–80

Independent variable	Initial productivity (residual)	Initial productivity (residual)
One or more ownership change	−0.0324 (6.42)	—
One ownership change	—	−0.0286 (5.28)
More than one change	—	−0.0532 (4.39)
Log plant employment, 1973	0.0050 (2.63)	0.0050 (2.62)
Intercept	0.0043 (2.36)	0.0043 (2.36)
Residual sum of squares	1,027.74	1,027.54
Residual degrees of freedom	18,224	18,223

Source: Author's calculations.
Note: t-statistics are in parentheses.

calculating them was not feasible. But Ravenscraft and Scherer concluded that profitability or performance of the line of business is the most important determinant of selling off a line of business. Similarly we find that productivity plays a major role in plant divestiture. Furthermore, unless the omitted variables are correlated with the regressors in the probit equation, our estimate of the impact of productivity on the decision to sell is unbiased.

Although we believe that low productivity leads to ownership change, another, perhaps more illuminating, way to examine this relationship is to compute the mean values of RELTFP73 by values of OC7480 (i.e., separately for plants that change and those that do not) and to test the hypothesis that the means are equal. Bergson (1987) used a similar methodology to estimate institutional differences in productivity between Communist bloc and Western mixed-economy countries. To control for the effects of plant size, we included employment as an additional regressor.[8] The point estimates, shown in table 3.3, are interpreted as measures of mean percentage difference in productivity between changers and nonchangers. The 1973 productivity of plants that changed owners between 1974 and 1980 was 3.2 percent lower than the productivity of plants that did not. Establishments that were destined to turn over more than once between 1974 and 1980 exhibited especially inferior performance in 1973.[9]

Table 3.4
Differences in mean levels of productivity between plants changing ownership in year t
and plants not changing ownership

Year	Level of productivity (residual)	Year	Level of productivity (residual)
$t - 7$	−2.6 (4.00)	$t + 1$	−2.9 (6.06)
$t - 6$	−3.0 (5.06)	$t + 2$	−2.7 (6.00)
$t - 5$	−3.4 (6.50)	$t + 3$	−2.5 (4.97)
$t - 4$	−3.3 (6.77)	$t + 4$	−1.9 (3.52)
$t - 3$	−3.3 (7.40)	$t + 5$	−1.9 (3.23)
$t - 2$	−3.6 (8.71)	$t + 6$	−1.8 (2.57)
$t - 1$	−3.7 (9.59)	$t + 7$	−1.2 (1.16)
t	−3.9 (9.10)		

Source: Author's calculations.
Note: t-statistics to test H_0: difference equals 0 are in parentheses.

Although the results of table 3.3 are instructive, they are based on a single cross section, and the ownership-change dummy variables are not year specific. For a more precise and comprehensive examination of the timing effects of ownership change, we computed productivity residuals based on Cobb-Douglas production functions, estimated separately by industry using annual data for 1973−80. These residuals were used to calculate differences in mean levels of productivity in year $t + i$ ($i = -7, -6, \ldots, 6, 7$) between plants changing owners in year t and plants remaining with the same corporation.[10] The pooled, within-industry ordinary least-squares estimates of these differences are presented in table 3.4. Consider the value −3.7 in year $t − 1$. This number indicates that plants changing owners in year t were 3.7 percent less productive in year $t − 1$ than plants in the same industry not changing owners in year t. The relative performance of changers in year t was poorest at the end of the transition year, the year of ownership change (−3.9 percent). Successive declines in the absolute values of the differences indicate that relative levels of efficiency improve after ownership changes.

Table 3.5
Regressions of growth in total-factor productivity on measures of ownership change, 1974–80

	Estimation technique								
	OLS	OLS	OLS	OLS	OLS	OLS	IV	IV	IV
At least one ownership change, 1974–80	0.0058 (4.77)	—	—	0.0042 (3.50)	—	—	0.0051 (4.29)	—	—
At least one ownership change, 1974–76	—	0.0090 (5.83)	—	—	0.0078 (5.15)	—	—	0.0084 (5.52)	—
At least one ownership change, 1977–80	—	0.0011 (0.64)	—	—	0.0008 (0.47)	—	—	0.0004 (0.27)	—
One ownership change, 1974–80	—	—	0.0054 (4.18)	—	—	0.0039 (3.06)	—	—	0.0048 (3.80)
More than one ownership change, 1974–80	—	—	0.0076 (2.60)	—	—	0.0056 (1.95)	—	—	0.0065 (2.27)
Initial productivity residual, 1974	—	—	—	−0.0452 (25.98)	−0.0453 (26.02)	−0.0452 (25.97)	−0.0327 (11.54)	−0.0327 (11.54)	−0.0326 (11.53)
Intercept	−0.0008 (1.75)	−0.0008 (1.73)	−0.0008 (1.75)	−0.0006 (1.32)	−0.0006 (1.27)	−0.0006 (1.29)	−0.0007 (1.58)	−0.0007 (1.57)	−0.0007 (1.57)
$\bar{R}^2$	58.94	58.90	58.91	56.88	56.84	56.84	57.04	57.00	56.00
Residual degrees of freedom	18,226	18,225	18,225	18,225	18,224	18,224	18,224	18,223	18,223

Source: Author's calculations, t-statistics in parentheses.
Note: OLS is ordinary least squares; IV is instrumental variables.

The other major implication of the matching theory is that plant turn-over should result in improvements in productivity. The values presented in table 3.4 suggest that productivity growth is higher after plants have been involved in takeovers. Just four years after ownership has changed, approximately 49 percent of the productivity gap that existed at $t - 1$ (-3.7 percent) between year t changers and nonchangers was closed (-1.9 percent). At $t + 7$ almost 68 percent of this gap was eliminated (-1.2 percent). Moreover the difference in $t + 7$ is not statistically significant. Thus we cannot reject the hypothesis that plants that were sold seven years before are just as productive as plants that were not sold.

To examine further the effects of plant turnover on economic efficiency, we computed regressions of the growth in TFP between 1974 and 1980 on various measures of the incidence of ownership change in those years. These results are reported in table 3.5, which supports the hypothesis that ownership change improves productivity. Plants involved in one or more transactions during this period experienced 0.58 percent higher TFP growth than their industry counterparts who remained with the same parent corporation.

If the new owners of plants increase the economic efficiency of these establishments, it seems likely that several years must elapse before this improvement is measurable. To test this assumption, we classified own-ership changes according to whether they occurred early (1974–76) or late (1977–80) in the period. Plants changing hands early had significant im-provements in efficiency; those changing toward the end of the period did not. Thus it appears that efficiency gains associated with ownership changes do not occur immediately. Productivity increases were slightly greater in plants that experienced more than one ownership change during the period.

Each plant's initial productivity is included in table 3.6 as an additional regressor to control for the possibility of regression toward the mean. As discussed previously, the increases in productivity that seem to be asso-ciated with a change in ownership may in fact reflect the tendency of below- or above-average values to regress toward mean values.

Plants that changed owners had lower initial levels of productivity and greater growth in productivity than plants that did not. Consistent with the matching hypothesis of plant turnover, we interpret the low initial level to be due to inefficient management (perhaps because of random mismatch) and the higher growth to be due on average to more efficient management. There are, however, at least two other potential explanations for the

Table 3.6
Differences in mean growth rates of output and inputs between plants changing owners in
year t and those not changing owners (percent)

Year	Output	Labor	Materials	Capital
$t - 7$	0.4	0.2	−0.9	−0.1
	(0.43)	(0.32)	(0.39)	(0.13)
$t - 6$	−0.3	−0.2	−0.8	−0.5
	(0.45)	(0.28)	(0.88)	(1.14)
$t - 5$	0.0	1.0	0.5	0.0
	(0.03)	(1.96)	(0.69)	(0.13)
$t - 4$	−1.2	−0.5	−1.0	0.0
	(2.09)	(0.96)	(1.59)	(0.18)
$t - 3$	−1.1	−0.4	−2.0	−0.5
	(2.06)	(0.78)	(2.77)	(1.71)
$t - 2$	−2.0	−0.8	−3.0	−0.7
	(4.03)	(2.01)	(5.03)	(2.79) ˙
$t - 1$	−2.4	−2.2	−3.3	−0.9
	(5.09)	(5.56)	(5.86)	(4.05)
t	−4.8	−4.1	−5.0	−0.6
	(9.42)	(10.65)	(8.15)	(2.90)
$t + 1$	1.3	0.4	0.1	1.0
	(2.49)	(1.00)	(0.16)	(4.51)
$t + 2$	1.5	1.0	0.8	0.2
	(2.81)	(2.26)	(1.26)	(0.79)
$t + 3$	1.3	0.6	1.4	0.6
	(1.95)	(1.31)	(1.93)	(2.58)
$t + 4$	0.8	−0.1	0.1	0.4
	(1.29)	(0.12)	(0.20)	(1.52)
$t + 5$	0.4	0.5	0.2	0.2
	(0.58)	(0.93)	(0.20)	(0.65)
$t + 6$	−0.6	−0.2	−1.0	0.2
	(0.74)	(0.37)	(1.10)	(0.70)
$t + 7$	−0.4	−0.4	−0.3	0.4
	(0.41)	(0.62)	(0.23)	(1.02)
Mean				
$t - 3$ to $t - 1$	−1.8	−1.1	−2.8	−0.7
$t + 1$ to $t + 3$	1.4	0.7	0.8	0.6

Source: Author's calculations.
Note: t-statistics to test H_0: difference equals 0 are in parentheses.

finding that plants with low initial productivity have higher subsequent productivity growth.

The first is the regression-to-the-mean hypothesis. Suppose that for behavioral reasons a plant's productivity growth is inversely related to its initial level so that

$$\text{TFP} - \text{TFP}_{-1} = \beta \text{TFP}_{-1} + e,$$

where e is a random disturbance. The equation may be rewritten as

$$\text{TFP} = (1 + \beta)\text{TFP}_{-1} + e = \alpha \text{TFP}_{-1} + e,$$

where $\alpha = (1 + \beta)$. The hypothesis is that $\beta < 0$ or that $\alpha < 1$. Plants beneath the frontier have opportunities to catch up; such opportunities are unavailable to "best-practice" plants near the frontier. In other words, all plants that exhibit substandard levels of performance at the beginning of a period can catch up, with or without changing owners.

The second potential explanation makes a weaker assumption about the evolution of TFP but is based on the fact that plants that close were not included in our sample. Suppose that TFP follows a random walk, that is, $\text{TFP} = \text{TFP}_{-1} + e$ so that (in the notation of the previous paragraph) $\alpha = 1$. Also assume that if a plant's relative productivity declines below a certain threshold, it will close. Consider the plants that experience a given decline in productivity from one year to the next. The higher its initial productivity, the less likely the plant is to cross the threshold and therefore to close. Plants with low initial levels of productivity are more likely to be absent from the sample than plants with high initial levels. Even if productivity follows a random walk, censoring could account for the fact that plants with low initial productivity levels have higher average productivity growth. Regression toward the mean could account for this fact even in the absence of censoring.

Neither of these mechanisms, however, could account for the entire set of coefficients presented in table 3.4. In particular, they cannot explain why the relative productivity of plants that change owners does not rise (and indeed falls) between $t - 7$ and t and rises only after t. Both the explanations sketched above would predict that relative productivity would increase, beginning in $t - 7$. The fact that productivity begins to rise only after the ownership change occurs strongly suggests that it is the change in ownership that is largely responsible for the improvement. When initial productivity is included in the regression model, the estimated coefficients decline, but only slightly. Thus even after controlling for a possible regression-to-the-mean effect, we still found that ownership change led to improvements in economic efficiency.

Finally, initial productivity may also have been mismeasured, perhaps because of errors in the industry deflators used to calculate constant dollar values of output, capital, materials, and energy. Measurement error is also associated with the calculation of levels of TFP. However, in constructing estimates of TFP growth, we assumed that this measurement error was permanent.[11] Thus the true model we attempt to estimate in column 4 of table 3.5 is of the form $y = \beta_1 X_1 + \beta_2 X_2 + u$, where y is TFP growth, X_1 is a (subsequent) ownership-change dummy variable X_2 is "true" initial productivity, and u is a classical disturbance term. We do not observe X_2, but rather an imperfect measure of initial productivity, $Z_2 = X_2 + \varepsilon$, where ε is a classical disturbance term. In addition, the measurement error ε is assumed to be uncorrelated with u and X_1. Griliches (1986) demonstrated that in the case of a regression model with two independent variables where only one is subject to measurement error, the bias in the point estimate of the variable that is measured incorrectly is transmitted to the other coefficient. He derived the following formula for the bias in b_1: $\text{plim}(b_1 - \beta_1) = -\pi \text{ (bias } b_2)$, where b_1 and b_2 are the OLS estimates of β_1 and β_2, respectively, and π is the correlation coefficient between X_1 and Z_2. We have already presented evidence suggesting that an inverse relationship exists between initial productivity and subsequent ownership change ($\pi < 0$). Furthermore it is well known that the ordinary least-squares (OLS) estimate of β_2 is biased toward zero.[12] Thus the bias in b_2 is transmitted to b_1, and we expect the OLS estimate of β_1 also to be biased toward zero. An instrumental variables (IV) estimator was used to adjust for the bias inherent in OLS estimation of the models in columns 4, 5, and 6 of table 3.5. We experimented with many possible instruments for initial productivity, settling on productivity in 1973 ($t - 7$) as the best instrument. As expected, the point estimates of the ownership-change dummies increased slightly, and their standard errors declined under two-stage least-squares estimation in columns 7, 8, and 9. Thus the efficiency-gain hypothesis associated with a matching theory of plant turnover was confirmed, even after adjusting for measurement error and a regression-to-the-mean effect.

The data are then consistent with the two key implications of the matching theory of ownership change, that the least-productive plants are most likely to change owners and that ownership change tends to be followed by above-average increases in productivity. Computing differences in mean growth rates of outputs, inputs, and productivity in year $t + i$ ($i = -7, -6, \ldots, 6, 7$) between plants changing owners in year t and plants not changing owners in year t provides additional insight into this phenomenon. As before, all data are standardized by four-digit SIC industry, so these differences should be interpreted as pooled, within-industry differences.[13] The differences and the associated t-statistics (for testing H_0: difference $= 0$) are presented in table 3.6. To clarify the interpretations of these numbers, consider the value -1.1 in the fifth row ($i = -3$) under "output." This value signifies that the mean rate of output growth in year $t - 3$ of firms that changed owners in year t was 1.1 percent lower than the corresponding mean output growth rate of year t nonchangers. In the output column the difference in growth rates is negative and generally increasing in magnitude from $t - 4$ through t, the year of ownership change, and is positive in years $t + 1$ to $t + 3$. All of these differences are statistically significant. The mean growth rate of output of year t changers was lower in every year before t except $t - 5$ and $t - 7$ (the average between $t - 3$ and $t - 1$ was -1.8 percent), and higher in every year between $t + 1$ and $t + 3$ (the average difference during this period was 1.4 percent). These differences show that change in ownership arrests and to some extent reverses the decline of a plant. Because the differences in output growth rates after ownership change are smaller than the differences before acquisition, the year t changers experienced a shrinking market share between years $t - 3$ and $t + 3$.

Consider next the differences in labor input growth rates. With one important exception, the pattern is similar to the case of output: From $t - 3$ through t the differences are negative and growing. Labor input begins to be higher for year t changers in $t + 1$, although the increases are smaller than they were for output growth. Still, the absence of lower growth rates after ownership change is inconsistent with the view that new owners seek significant reductions in employment. Shleifer and Summers suggest that a firm's long-term implicit contracts with workers and suppliers are breached in the course of a hostile takeover. Our analysis indicates that changes in ownership are more likely to stem employment reductions than trigger mass layoffs (see Shleifer and Summers 1987).[14] The statistics for materials tell a similar story: dramatically slower growth in materials used and in capital before and during the ownership change, and slightly higher growth afterward.

The differences in annual total factor productivity growth rates are inconsistent with the results reported earlier and with input and outputs. Plants that were sold had significantly higher TFP growth in years $t - 1$ through $t + 1$. We believe these results are implausible because TFP growth is calculated as output growth minus a Divisia index of input growth, using plant-specific factor shares as weights. Short-term fluctuations in plant activities are such that factor shares and thus TFP growth rates are computed imprecisely.

Conclusions

In the sample 21 percent of plants that are larger than average manufacturing establishments experienced at least one change in corporate control between 1972 and 1981. Evidence pertaining to the determinants and effects of these transfers is consistent with the empirical implications of a matching theory of plant turnover. That is, a firm lacking a comparative advantage with respect to a given plant will sell it to another corporation, leading on average to an improvement in the plant's economic performance.

Our analysis of the factors influencing divestitures of plants found that low levels of efficiency increase the likelihood of ownership change. A probit regression of subsequent turnover on initial productivity and size revealed that industry laggards in 1973 were more likely to be sold in the following six years than plants that were efficient. The suitability of matches between plants and firms thus seem to be rationally evaluated by their owners. Low levels of productivity indicate that a plant and its owner are not suited for each other, and a termination of this relationship is imminent. In the previous section we presented prima facie evidence of improvement in the efficiency of manufacturing plants after changes in corporate ownership. In our framework efficiency gains were defined as higher rates of TFP growth, or larger movements toward the production frontiers by establishments changing owners. Plants involved in ownership changes experienced, on average, 0.5 percent higher TFP growth between 1974 and 1980, a result driven by the 0.8 percent increase realized by plants changing hands during the first three years in the six-year period. Apparently it takes several years for a new parent to have a significant influence on performance.

Results concerning differences in levels of productivity between sold and unsold plants (table 3.4) provide the most powerful evidence supporting the hypothesis of increased efficiency. Sold plants exhibit both lower initial levels of productivity and a deterioration in relative performance through the year in which these acquisitions occur. But after changing owners, their improvement in performance reduces and eventually (after seven years) almost eliminates the productivity gap that existed between them and the control group before takeover. Truncation or censoring caused by our failure to observe plants that close cannot explain these patterns of relative performance, but it would be desirable to confirm this claim by analyzing uncensored data. This is a task for future research.[15]

The years covered in our analysis may explain the divergence of the findings from those of Ravenscraft and Scherer (1986), who contended that mergers are bad for the economy. Using the Federal Trade Commision's line-of-business data, they concluded that lines of business acquired during the 1960s and early 1970s were highly profitable before mergers but experienced declining profitability afterward. Given that the line-of-business sample consists mainly of large, diversified corporations (approximately 470 firms), many of these transactions were conglomerate mergers and acquisitions. In a subsequent paper they observed that heightened merger activity in the 1960s led to massive divestitures in the 1970s, divestitures that were precipitated by steadily deteriorating profits (see Ravenscraft and Scherer 1986). Observing 282 lines of business before and after divestiture (line-of-business data are available for 1974–77), they concluded that these units earned higher profits after being acquired by new corporations but that performance did not improve enough to allow them to earn normal rates of return. The results of that paper are generally consistent with our findings. However, Ravenscraft and Scherer would argue that changes in ownership in the 1970s generally yielded improvements in efficiency because most of the transactions involved spin-offs of previously acquired and unrelated lines of business. According to this view a wave of unwarranted acquisitions in the 1960s led to disappointing performance and large numbers of sell-offs in the 1970s.

Still, our findings concerning the determinants and effects of plant turnover imply that ownership change plays an important role in redeeming inefficient plants. In *Exit, Voice and Loyalty* Hirschman (1970, 1) argued that some agents in an economic system may experience lapses from efficient or rational behavior. If the system functions smoothly, forces exist that will rectify this inefficient activity:

No matter how well a society's basic institutions are devised, failures of some actors to live up to the behavior which is expected of them are bound to occur, if only for all kinds of accidental reasons. Each society learns to live with a certain amount of dysfunctional or misbehavior; but lest the misbehavior feed on itself and lead to general decay, society must be able to marshal from within itself forces which will make as many of the faltering actors as possible revert to the behavior required for its proper functioning.

Our evidence is consistent with the view that ownership change or asset redeployment is an important mechanism for correcting lapses from inefficient producer behavior. The gains realized by both target and acquiring shareholders appear to be social gains, not merely private ones. We found no evidence that ownership change is usually accompanied by the abrogation of implicit contracts with workers or suppliers.

The often-cited productivity slowdown in the 1970s was reflected in our sample. The average TFP growth for all plants in the sample from 1974 to 1980 was −0.3 percent. Our evidence strongly suggested that this deterioration would have been more pronounced if ownership changes had not transpired. These results imply that policymakers should be extremely cautious when considering policies that would make ownership change more difficult or costly.

4

Takeovers and Corporate Overhead

with Donald Siegel

One view of the process of ownership change is that takeovers (actual or threatened) are often necessary to force or allow significant changes in management practices, particularly substantial curtailment in (some of) the firm's activities. Shleifer and Vishny (1988, 11), for example, argue that "hostile takeovers affect industries in decline or sharp change where managers fail to shrink operations rapidly enough or to make other adjustments. In maintaining full-scale operations, managers may be guarding the domain of their control or trying to protect employees from dismissal or wage cuts." The group of employees that top executives may try hardest to protect are their immediate subordinates: managers and administrators employed at corporate or divisional headquarters. If so, a change in ownership would have a much greater impact on these employees than it would have on those lower down in the corporate hierarchy.

Prominent corporate "raiders" claim that this is indeed the case. Henry Kravis (1989, 71) makes the following statements concerning leveraged buyouts:

People who produce things will stay. We look at the people who report to people who report to people. We'll often cut fat at the corporate level. There'd be much less of this ... if chief executives felt the pressure from their directors to do the cutting that they only do when they're threatened by takeover.

In a similar vein Carl Icahn (1989) asserts that we have

created a corporate welfare state ... companies are burdened by layers of vice presidents who not only don't produce, but are often counterproductive.... I and other "raiders" usually eliminate the people who are most responsible for the mess—the "Top Brass".... In 1986, I took control of T.W.A ... and managed to eliminate more than $300 million a year in waste and bureaucracy.

The $25 billion leveraged buyout in 1989 of RJR Nabisco by Kohlberg Kravis Roberts—the largest takeover in history—provides a graphic example of this process. In the early summer of 1989, after the buyout, the company's headquarters was moved and its staff reduced from 650 to 350. In August 1989 the tobacco unit of the firm announced it would dismiss 825 white-collar workers and 700 manufacturing employees. Since the initial number of white-collar workers was undoubtedly much smaller, this must have substantially reduced the ratio of white-collar to manufacturing employment. The chief executive of the unit explained that "management layers were being wiped out in a streamlining process" and that "five daily mail deliveries were cut back to two and four engineering groups were consolidated into one."[1]

This kind of "restructuring" can occur in the absence of a major shock to the organization, such as a takeover or bankruptcy. General Electric and Monsanto provide two recent examples of this:

[The chief executive of General Electric turned] GE from a textbook case of a massive, bureaucratically managed conglomerate into a new model of decentralised, liberated management.... He has dispensed with layers of headquarters staff, cutting it from 1700 to 1000 by removing the administrators that acted as filters between each business unit and the boss's office....

Monsanto's main organisational change in its factories has been to do away with most of its foremen, supervisors, and quality inspectors and instead to invite plant workers to oversee themselves.... Another useful change has been to give workers contact with their customers, so that they know where the product goes and why.... Previously, they would have gone through the sales staff.[2]

Although these specific reductions in administrative overhead occurred in the absence of takeovers, we hypothesize that in general such reductions are much more likely to occur in firms experiencing changes in corporate control than in other firms.

In this chapter we test this and other hypotheses by providing estimates of the effects of takeovers on the employment and wages of employees in both auxiliary establishments (which include central administrative offices) and production establishments. These estimates are obtained via econometric analysis of large longitudinal data sets based on Census Bureau surveys of both types of establishments. For each establishment type we estimate the differences between changing and not changing owners in the growth of employment and wages. In this way we can contrast the effects of takeovers on auxiliary- and production-establishment employees. We can also identify the effects on a small but important subset of employees engaged in research and development (R&D) and distinguish between the effects on production and nonproduction workers.

There is a small previous literature on the labor impact of ownership change, but no previous studies have examined administrative employment separately. In the next section we briefly review the existing evidence.

Previous Research on the Labor Impact of Ownership Change

We are aware of two previous studies that provide evidence concerning the labor impact of ownership change. Both studies examined firm- or plant-level data. The first is Kaplan's (1988) analysis of a sample of 33 large (over $50 million) management buyouts of public companies completed between 1980 and 1986. Kaplan compared the number of employees at the end of the first full postbuyout year in which employment numbers were reported with the number of employees in the year before the buyout.[3] He found that the median employment change for all 33 firms was zero but that the median industry-adjusted employment change was − 15.3 percent. In other words, employment growth among buyout firms was 15.3 percentage points below growth among nonbuyout firms in the same industry. When he restricted the analysis to 22 firms not engaged in extensive postbuyout acquisition and divestiture activity, the raw and industry-adjusted median employment changes were 3.3 percent and − 11.4 percent, respectively. Thus Kaplan's much smaller and more narrowly focused data set revealed declines in relative employment about two to three times greater than ours did (table 3.6) and over a narrower event window.

The second study of ownership change is by Brown and Medoff (1988). Its principal focus is on its effects on labor, and it provides estimates of wage effects as well. These authors analyzed quarterly employment and payroll data contained in unemployment insurance records kept by the Michigan Employment Security Commission. As they acknowledge, an important disadvantage of this data set is that it covers only a single state. Consequently the data do not reflect what is happening in other locations of multistate companies, and few large acquisitions are recorded in their data. Brown and Medoff distinguished three kinds of ownership change: (1) simple sales where firm A changes ownership without being integrated with any other firm, (2) assets-only sales where firm A purchases the assets of firm B without absorbing its work force, and (3) merger where firm A purchases firm B and at least initially absorbs most of firm B's workers (or firm A and firm B combine to form firm C, with at least initially firm C including most of the workers of firms A and B). Their estimates of the employment and wage changes associated with each type of transaction are as follows:

	Percent employment change	Percent wage change
Simple sale	+9	−5
Assets-only sale	−5	+5
Merger	+2	−4

Farber (1988) observed that the fact that transactions were classified on the basis of employment changes makes it difficult to interpret the employment effects. Brown and Medoff, however, acknowledge that the estimates of these effects are sensitive to specification details; the wage effects were less ambiguous. Because only about one-third of these transactions were assets-only sales, their estimates imply that on average wages fall slightly (about 1 or 2 percent) in connection with ownership change. They observe that in mergers the wage decline may partly be due to the departure of the relatively highly paid head of the acquired firm.

Auerbach (1988, 2) suggested that perhaps the most important conclusion that can be drawn from the Brown and Medoff study is that the employment and wage changes associated with ownership change are of relatively small magnitude. But even if the effect of ownership change on overall employment and wage rates is small, it may have a sizable impact on the employment and wage of specific types of workers. Our data enable us to determine the effects of ownership change on a relatively small, but important, subset of employees who work in auxiliary establishments where many top managers, administrators, and R&D personnel are based.

Data and Descriptive Statistics

For our empirical analysis we use three distinct data sets, each based on a different Census Bureau census or survey of establishments or firms. The first data set is collected from the Auxiliary Establishment Reports of the 1977 and 1982 economic censuses. Researchers have not, to our knowledge, previously analyzed these data at the micro level. The Census Bureau defines auxiliary establishments as those primarily engaged in support services for company divisions or other companies and the general public, including general and business administration, management, R&D, warehousing, and electronic data processing.[4] The census of auxiliary establishments collects data on the number of employees, by type of work performed, annual payroll, depreciable assets, capital expenditures, and other variables and attributes of the establishment. In 1982 there were almost

Table 4.1
Distribution of auxiliary-establishment employees by type of work performed, all
industries, 1982

Type of work performed	Number of employees	Percent of all employees
Administrative and managerial	906	35.3
Office and clerical	663	25.8
Research, development, and testing	240	9.3
Warehousing	268	10.4
Electronic data processing	134	5.2
Direct sales to customers	73	6.1
Other activities	85	7.9
Total	2570	100.0

Note: Number of employees is in thousands.

36,000 auxiliary establishments, and almost 2.6 million people were employed in them. Table 4.1 shows the 1982 distribution of auxiliary establishment employees by type of work performed. About one-third of employees are classified as administrative and managerial.[5] The principal activity of 9.3 percent (240 thousand) of these employees was research, development, and testing.[6]

We obtained data for the entire set of auxiliary establishments in the two adjacent census years 1977 and 1982. When records for a given establishment (identified by a unique establishment code) were present in both years, we linked them together.[7] Each record also contains a code identifying the parent company that owns the establishment. We assumed that the establishment's owner changed if and only if there was a change in the value of this code between 1977 and 1982. This procedure is probably subject to both type I and type II errors: Some nonmatches of the code may be due to coding errors, and certain ownership changes may not result in changes in the code. Measurement error contained in our indicator of ownership change is likely to bias toward zero the estimated differences in behavior between establishments changing and not changing owners. Unfortunately, the data do not permit us to classify ownership changes into different types, such as hostile versus friendly takeovers.

The data set described above enables us to contrast the employment and wage behavior of auxiliary establishments changing owners with that of auxiliary establishments not changing owners. We also wish to contrast the former with the behavior of production establishments changing owners. To accomplish this, we utilize the Longitudinal Research Database (LRD) described in chapter 2 and analyzed in chapter 3.

Table 4.2 presents data on the aggregate employment and payroll of both auxiliary and production establishments in manufacturing, for census years from 1947 to 1982. Auxiliary-establishment employment grew more rapidly than production-establishment employment. The number of auxiliary-establishment employees per 100 production-establishment employees increased from 2.0 in 1947 to 7.2 in 1982. Payroll per employee is much higher in auxiliary than in production establishments. The gap increased considerably from 1947 to 1963 but has narrowed somewhat since then.

Empirical Analysis of the Effects of Takeovers

We begin our empirical analysis of the labor impact of ownership change by considering the data presented in table 4.3 on mean and median values of employment and wage levels and changes, 1977–82, by status of auxiliary establishment.[8] The four mutually exclusive statuses and the criteria for assigning them to auxiliary establishments were as follows: (1) no change if the establishment was present in both 1977 and 1982 censuses and had the same owner ID, (2) changed owners if the establishment was present in both years and had different IDs, (3) closed if the establishment was present in 1977 only, and (4) opened if the establishment was present in 1982 only. Previous studies have documented the high rate of closing and opening of production establishments between census years. For example, Dunne, Roberts, and Samuelson (1988, Table 1b) estimated that 25 to 40 percent (depending on plant age) of the manufacturing establishments present in a given census had closed by the next census. Table 4.3 indicates that a similar "failure rate" (36.3 percent in manufacturing) applies to auxiliary establishments. Also as in the case of production establishments, auxiliary establishments that close are smaller on average than those that survive.

The number of establishments closing and opening is large relative to the number of surviving establishments, and very large relative to the number changing owners. But because we observe establishments that close or open only once, we cannot compare their employment or wage changes with those of surviving plants. In the remainder of this section we will analyze only the data on surviving establishments. Later in this chapter we discuss the possibility of bias due to censoring of establishments.[9]

The surviving establishments that changed owners had lower mean employment and wages (but higher median employment) than those that did not. Among the surviving establishments, 10.5 percent of the auxiliary establishments and 10.8 percent of establishments in manufacturing changed

Table 4.2
Employment and payroll of auxiliary and production establishments in manufacturing, 1947–82

Year	(1) Auxiliary establishments Employment	(2) Payroll	(3) Payroll per employee	(4) Production establishments Employment	(5) Payroll	(6) Payroll per employee	(7) (1)/(4) (percent)	(8) (3)/(6) (percent)
1947	300	1,200	4.0	14,900	41,200	2.8	2.0	1.43
1954	500	3,000	6.0	15,700	63,300	4.0	3.2	1.50
1958	600	4,400	7.3	15,400	73,900	4.8	3.9	1.53
1963	727	6,600	9.6	16,232	93,300	5.7	4.5	1.68
1967	831	8,700	10.8	18,492	123,500	6.7	4.5	1.61
1972	994	13,700	14.1	18,034	160,400	8.9	5.5	1.58
1977	1,074	22,000	20.5	18,516	242,000	13.1	5.8	1.57
1982	1,276	38,000	29.8	17,818	341,000	19.1	7.2	1.56

Source: U.S. Bureau of the Census, 1982 Census of Manufactures, Subject Series MC82-S-1 (Part 1), General Summary, p. 1–98. 1977 Census of Manufactures, Subject Series MC77-SR-14, Indexes of Production, p. 14–2.
Note: Employment is in thousands, payroll in millions of dollars, and payroll per employee in thousands of dollars.

Table 4.3
Mean and median values of employment and wage levels and changes, by status of auxiliary establishment, 1977–82

Status	N	Employment		Change in ln(emp), 1977–82	Wage		Change in ln(wage), 1977–82
		1977	1982		1977	1982	
All industries							
No change	16,730	93.2	99.6	0.031	17.6	26.8	0.397
		(17)	(17)	(0)	(15.3)	(24.5)	(0.394)
Changed owners	2,027	57.9	63.2	−0.158	14.7	22.1	0.392
		(12)	(10)	(−0.074)	(13.1)	(20.3)	(0.390)
Closed	12,184	34.0	—	—	15.7	—	—
		(10)			(143)		
Opened	17,219	—	45.0	—	—	27.0	—
			(13)			(25.1)	
Manufacturing							
No change	5,390	156.3	174.3	0.042	20.0	30.1	0.398
		(30)	(31)	(0)	(17.9)	(26.3)	(0.400)
Changed owners	633	93.2	101.0	−0.120	18.6	26.8	0.354
		(36)	(31)	(−0.072)	(16.5)	(25.0)	(0.394)
Closed	3,437	52.5	—	—	17.6	—	—
		(14)			(15.1)		
Opened	4,134	—	65.3	—	—	29.0	—
			(18)			(25.7)	

Note: Employment is number of workers, and wage is payroll per employee, in thousands of dollars. Medians are reported in parentheses below means.

owners. To calculate the percent of employees affected by changes in ownership, we can weight the number of establishments by their respective mean employment; in manufacturing the proportion of employees affected is 6.5 percent.[10]

Perhaps the most interesting statistics in table 4.3 are the mean growth rates (changes in logarithms) of employment and wages. Mean employment growth in auxiliary establishments that changed owners was 19 percent lower (16 percent in the case of manufacturing establishments) than it was in establishments that did not change owners. Establishments that did not change owners experienced modest positive growth; those that did change owners experienced sharp declines in employment. Establishments changing owners also had lower growth rates of nominal wages, although only in the case of manufacturing establishments is the difference nonnegligible—4.4 percentage points.[11]

The differences between growth rates are interesting and suggestive, but for at least two reasons one might believe that the simple differences are biased estimates of the true effects of ownership change. First, the data analyzed in table 4.3 were not standardized by industry. If the incidence of ownership change is greater in industries with above- or below-average employment growth, then differences between unstandardized growth rates may provide a distorted picture of the impact of ownership change on employment. Blair (1988) found that the level of merger activity tends to be higher in industries experiencing lower employment growth, suggesting that the estimates reported above overstate the industry-adjusted differential.

Second, it is well known that there is a strong negative correlation between the initial size of firms and their subsequent growth rates. Hall (1987, 603) has recently shown that "neither measurement error in employment nor sample attrition can account for the negative coefficient on firm size in the growth rate equation." Since establishments changing owners are smaller than those not changing owners, in the absence of any effect of ownership change on employment growth one would expect the former to exhibit higher employment growth. The employment-growth differences shown in table 4.3 would therefore underestimate the effect of ownership change.

We can eliminate both of the potential biases (which may be offsetting) by estimating regression models of the form

$$\ln X_{ijt} = \beta_1 OC_{ijt} + \beta_2 \ln X_{ijt-5} + \gamma_j + u_{ijt}, \tag{1}$$

where X denotes either employment or wages, the subscript ijt refers to establishment i in four-digit SIC industry j in year t, OC equals 1 if the establishment changed owners between $t - 5$ and t and otherwise equals zero, and u is a classical disturbance. Simply comparing the growth rates of establishments changing and not changing owners is equivalent to imposing the restrictions $\beta_2 = 1$ and $\gamma_j = \gamma$, $\forall_j$. We now relax those restrictions.

Estimates of the parameter β_1 in equation (1) for auxiliary establishments in all industries and in manufacturing and production establishments in manufacturing are reported in table 4.4. Relaxing the restrictions reduces slightly the estimated employment effect of changes in ownership of auxiliary establishments: The mean relative employment of establishments changing owners declines about 16 to 17 percent. In contrast, relaxing the restrictions has a substantial impact on the estimated wage effects: Controlling for industry and the initial wage level, mean wage growth of auxiliary establishments changing owners is 9.2 percentage points lower (6.0 per-

Table 4.4
Estimated effects of ownership change on employment and wage in auxiliary and production establishments

Type of establishment	Industry	Effect of ownership change on:		N
		Employment	Wage	
Auxiliary	All	−0.167 (8.4)	−0.092 (7.3)	18,448
Auxiliary	Manufacturing	−0.157 (4.6)	−0.060 (3.3)	5,949
Production	Manufacturing	−0.045 (5.4)	−0.021 (4.7)	18,586

Note: Each of the effects reported is an estimate of the coefficient β_1 in a regression of the form

$$\ln X_{ijt} = \beta_1 OC_{ijt} + \beta_2 \ln X_{ijt-5} + \gamma_j + u_{ijt},$$

where X denotes either employment or the wage rate, the subscript ijt refers to establishment i in industry j in year t, OC equals 1 if the establishment changed owners between $t-5$ and t and equals zero otherwise, γ_j is a "fixed effect" for industry j, and u is a classical disturbance. For auxiliary establishments t is 1982, and for production establishments is 1981. All equations included a complete set of four-digit SIC industry dummy variables. Numbers in parentheses are t-statistics.

centage points in manufacturing) than that of establishments not changing owners. These estimates imply that employment and real wages fell significantly more in auxiliary establishments changing owners between 1977 and 1982 than in those that did not. The growth in total payroll was 25.0 percentage points lower in auxiliary establishments changing owners.

In addition to estimating the effect of ownership change on the total employment of auxiliary establishments, we can also estimate the effect on R&D employment for a subset of establishments. This would include the number of persons whose principal activity is research, development, and testing. As Auerbach (1988, 3–4) notes, some parties to the popular and policy debates about takeovers are concerned that takeovers, actual or threatened, may reduce investment in long-term projects, particularly R&D. Defining X as R&D employment, we have estimated equation (1) for the subset of 1099 establishments in all industries that reported positive values of this variable in both years.[12] The point estimate (t-statistic) for β_1 from this equation is −0.039 (0.5). The estimate is less than one-fourth as large in magnitude as the corresponding estimate for total employment, and it is far from statistically significant. Hence we cannot reject the null hypothesis of no difference between establishments changing and not changing owners in the growth of R&D employment. This finding is consistent with that of Hall (1988) who "found very little evidence in the existing data (through 1985) that acquisitions cause a reduction in R&D spending; in the aggregate, firms involved in mergers showed no difference in their pre- and post-merger R&D performance over those not so involved."

To contrast the effects of ownership change on auxiliary establishments with its effects on production establishments, we also estimated equation (1) using the LRD for production establishments.[13] The results are shown in the last line of table 4.4. Ownership change is associated with relative declines in employment and wages in production establishments, but the magnitudes of the declines are only about one-third those for auxiliary establishments. Controlling for industry and initial size, the growth rate of employment is 4.5 percentage points lower for production establishments changing owners between 1976 and 1981 than it is for other production establishments. As noted earlier, production establishments changing owners tend to have higher employment growth in the first several years after ownership change than production establishments that have not changed owners; the negative net effect of ownership change on five-year employment growth is due to large relative employment declines immediately preceding the change.

Because we observe auxiliary establishments only twice, we cannot determine for them the extent to which the decline in relative employment and wages occurs before rather than after ownership change. But the much greater net decline in auxiliary establishments is still informative: Even if the reductions in auxiliary establishments occurred prior to ownership change, the data reveal that the new owners elected not to reverse the reductions nearly as much as they did in production establishments.

The wage effects shown in table 4.4 are based on the definition of the wage as payroll per employee, so supplementary labor compensation is excluded. In the case of production establishments, we were also able to estimate the model for X defined as total compensation (payroll plus supplementary compensation) per employee. Using this more comprehensive wage measure changes the estimated wage effect β_1 (and its t-statistic) from -0.021 (4.7) to -0.029 (7.8). The relative decline in total compensation per employee is 38 percent greater than the relative decline in payroll per employee. Because the ratio of aggregate supplementary labor compensation to aggregate total compensation is about 0.2, this implies that the effect of ownership change on supplements per employee is -0.061, about three times as great as its effect on payroll per employee.

The difference between the employment effect of ownership change in auxiliary and production establishments has some interesting and important implications. Let Δ represent the difference between establishments changing and not changing owners, A represent auxiliary-establishment employment, P represent production-establishment employment, and R represent their ratio A/P. The dot over the letters indicate growth rates. Then

$$\Delta\dot{R} = \Delta\dot{A} - \Delta\dot{P} = -0.157 - (-0.045) = -0.112.$$

Therefore ownership change reduces the ratio of auxiliary-establishment employment to production establishment employment by 11.2 percent. As table 4.1 shows, the simple average of the 1977 and 1982 aggregate values of this ratio is $(5.8 + 7.2)/2 = 6.4$ percent. Evaluated at this population mean, the 11.2 percent reduction in R implies the elimination of about 7.2 auxiliary establishment jobs for every 1,000 production establishment jobs. This reduction in R is consistent with the examples of restructuring described earlier in the chapter.

The measure of labor input we used in chapter 3's analysis of the effects of ownership change on total-factor productivity did not account for auxiliary establishment employment; it was based only on production establishment employment. Since ownership change results in a reduction in R, we underestimated the true relative decline in labor input, and the true relative increase in TFP, that occurs in connection with ownership change. The difference in the growth in true labor input L^* is

$$\Delta\dot{L}^* = S_A\Delta\dot{A} + (1 - S_A)\Delta\dot{P}$$

$$= \Delta\dot{P} + S_A(\Delta\dot{A} - \Delta\dot{P})$$

$$= \Delta\dot{P} + S_A\Delta\dot{R},$$

where S_A is the share of auxiliary establishment payroll in total (auxiliary-plus production-establishment) payroll. The mean of the 1977 and 1982 aggregate values of S_A is equal to 9.2 percent.

Before our measure of labor input growth was simply $\dot{P}$; the error e in our measure was

$$e = \Delta\dot{L}^* - \Delta\dot{P} = S_A\Delta\dot{R} = (0.092)(-0.112) = -0.0103.$$

Since $\Delta\dot{P} = -0.045$, this represents a percentage error of about 23 percent. To assess the resulting error in the estimate of the effect of ownership change on TFP growth, we need merely to multiply e by (-1 times) labor's share in gross output, which is approximately 0.34. Because true relative labor input fell 1.03 percentage points more than we had estimated, true relative TFP increased 0.34 percentage points more than we had estimated. We had previously estimated that ownership change is associated with relative TFP increases of 0.42 to 0.51 percentage points. Thus when we properly account for changes in auxiliary-establishment employment, our estimate of the effect of ownership change on TFP is increased about 75 percent, from 0.46 to 0.80 percentage points.

Up until now we have been analyzing one kind of relative-employment effect of ownership change: its effect on the ratio of auxiliary-establishment employment to production-establishment employment. As we noted earlier, the census data enable us to distinguish between two different types of employees in production establishments: production and nonproduction workers. About one-fourth of production-establishment employees are nonproduction workers. In their work and their earning (skill) levels, nonproduction workers in production establishments (denoted NP) may be closer to auxiliary-establishment employees (denoted A) than they are to production employees in production establishments (denoted PP).[14] We therefore consider the effect of ownership change on the ratio NP/PP and also on (NP + A)/PP.[15]

Because we have annual rather than merely quinquennial data on production establishments, our method of analysis will differ slightly from the one developed earlier. Our procedure is to estimate regressions of the form

$$\ln X_{ij,t+k} = \beta_k OC_{ijt} + \gamma_j + u_{ij,t+k},$$

where X denotes $P(=\text{PP} + \text{NP})$, PP, or NP; the subscripts ij, $t + k$ denote establishment i in industry j in year $t + k$ ($k = -5, -4, \ldots, -3, +4$); OC_{ijt} equals 1 if the establishment changed owners between $t - 1$ and t, and otherwise equals zero; j is a "fixed effect" for industry j; and u is a classical disturbance. Hence β_k is the percentage difference in the mean value of X in year $t + k$ between establishments changing and not changing owners between $t - 1$ and t. Estimates of the β_k are reported in table 4.5. The figure -0.082 in the first row and column indicates that establishments that will change owners between four and five years later on average employ 8.2 percent fewer workers than those that will not change owners. As in the case of auxiliary establishments, the probability of future ownership change is inversely related to current size. The first column clearly documents the fact noted earlier that the relative total employment of plants changing owners declines sharply until immediately after the change and then increases slightly.[16]

Table 4.5
Differences in mean log employment (total, production, and nonproduction) in year $t + k$ between production establishments changing and not changing owners between $t - 1$ and t

Year	Total employment (PP + NP)	Production-worker employment (PP)	Nonproduction-worker employment (NP)
$t - 5$	−0.069	−0.082	0.012
	(3.68)	(4.24)	(1.95)
$t - 4$	−0.072	−0.086	0.013
	(4.11)	(4.79)	(2.45)
$t - 3$	−0.072	−0.082	0.010
	(4.41)	(4.95)	(1.97)
$t - 2$	−0.103	−0.116	0.017
	(6.89)	(7.61)	(3.62)
$t - 1$	−0.119	−0.133	0.012
	(8.03)	(8.81)	(2.61)
t	−0.132	−0.153	0.012
	(9.48)	(10.73)	(2.66)
$t + 1$	−0.131	−0.145	0.012
	(8.67)	(9.33)	(2.39)
$t + 2$	−0.120	−0.131	0.009
	(7.28)	(7.78)	(1.76)
$t + 3$	−0.118	−0.125	0.011
	(6.72)	(6.69)	(1.88)
$t + 4$	−0.124	−0.126	0.015
	(6.54)	(5.97)	(2.38)

As columns 2 and 3 of table 4.5 show, the data on total employment mask very different patterns for production and nonproduction employment. Whereas plants changing owners on average employ 7 to 13 percent fewer production workers than plants not changing owners in every year from $t - 5$ to $t + 4$, they employ 1 to 2 percent more nonproduction workers in every year, and the differences are mostly significant. The ratio of nonproduction to production employees is 9 to 16 percent higher in plants changing owners. Moreover, the decline in relative employment prior to ownership change, and the partial subsequent recovery, is confined almost entirely to production-worker employment. There is very little movement over time in the relative employment of nonproduction workers.

To obtain estimates of the effects of ownership change on PP and NP workers that are comparable to our estimates of the effects on A workers, we compute averages of the 5 five-year differences $\beta_0 - \beta_{-5}$, $\beta_1 - \beta_{-4}$, ..., $\beta_4 - \beta_{-1}$. Estimates of the effect of ownership change on five-year relative-employment growth, for PP, NP, and A, are as follows:

Type of worker	Estimate
PP	−0.036
NP	−0.001
A	−0.157

Whereas the relative decline in A associated with ownership change is apparently much greater than the relative decline in PP, the relative decline in NP is essentially zero. In 1982 there were 10.3 A workers and 43.7 NP workers per 100 PP workers in manufacturing, so the mean value of the fraction $a = A/(A + NP)$ is 0.191. Hence the relative decline in the sum $S = A + NP$ is

$$\Delta\dot{S} = a\Delta\dot{A} + (1 - a)\Delta\dot{NP} = -0.030,$$

which is close to, indeed slightly less than, the mean relative decline in production-worker employment $\Delta\dot{P} = -0.035$. Although the ratio of auxiliary-establishment employees to production workers declines sharply in connection with ownership change, the ratio of total "indirect" labor (A + NP) to "direct" labor (PP) does not (in fact it appears to increase slightly) due to the negligible effect of ownership change on the employment level of nonproduction workers in production establishments.

Takeover-Related Transfers of Employees between Auxiliary Establishments

In the previous section we presented evidence that the difference in employment (and wage) growth rates between auxiliary establishments changing and not changing owners was negative, and much more negative than the corresponding difference for production establishments. We interpreted this to signify that ownership change is associated with sharp reductions in the firm's employment of auxiliary establishment personnel, relative to its employment of production establishment personnel. It is possible, however, that when a firm that already owns an auxiliary establishment acquires another auxiliary establishment, it transfers employees from the acquired to the existing establishment, or vice versa. Some individuals have expressed to us their belief that transfers of personnel from acquired to existing administrative offices are common, although we are not aware of any reliable evidence on this issue. If this is the case, then we may have overestimated in the previous section the reductions in R associated with changes in ownership, since the employment declines in acquired establishments would be offset by employment increases in other establishments owned by the acquiring firm.

In this section we attempt to address the issue of employee transfer in two alternative ways, both of which account for employment in nonacquired auxiliaries owned by firms acquiring other auxiliaries. The first way is to extend table 4.3 by cross-classifying (surviving) establishments by (1) whether they changed owners and (2) whether the parent of the establishment in 1982 owned other auxiliary establishments. The second way is to calculate the auxiliary intensity (the ratio of auxiliary establishment employment to total company employment) at the firm level in both 1977 and 1982 and to determine the mean change from 1977 to 1982 in the parent's auxiliary intensity by whether the auxiliary establishment changed owners.

To implement the first approach, we constructed a dummy variable (OTH82) equal to 1 if the 1982 parent of the auxiliary establishment owned other auxiliary establishments in 1982, and otherwise equal to zero. Table 4.6 reports both the number of auxiliary establishments and the mean 1977–82 change in log employment of auxiliary establishments, cross-classified by OTH82 and OC. (Recall that the latter variable equals 1 if the establishment changed owners between 1977 and 1982, and otherwise equals zero.) The top panel reveals that only 24 percent (469/1,982) of establishments changing owners were owned by parents that owned multiple auxiliaries in 1982, whereas 67 percent (10,997/16,467) of establishments not changing owners were multiple-auxiliary establishments. Thus the possibility of transferring employees from acquired to existing

Table 4.6
Number and mean change in log employment of auxiliary establishments, cross-classified by OTH82 and OC

	$OC = 0$	$OC = 1$	All
Number of auxiliary establishments			
OTH82 = 0	5,470	1,513	6,983
OTH82 = 1	10,997	469	11,466
All	16,467	1,982	18,449
Mean 1977–82 change in log employment			
OTH82 = 0	−0.027	−0.120	−0.047
OTH82 = 1	0.060	−0.279	0.046
All	0.031	−0.158	0.011

establishments exists in the case of only about one-fourth of acquired establishments. The first line of the bottom panel of the table reveals that there are substantial declines in employment among establishments changing owners (both absolute and relative to establishments not changing owners) even if they were acquired by firms that did not own other auxiliaries in 1982. The absolute and relative rates of employment growth were -0.120 and -0.093, respectively. Thus the transfer hypothesis cannot entirely account for the results of the previous section. But the second line of the bottom panel indicates that the absolute and relative employment declines of plants changing owners are much greater if the acquiring firm owned other auxiliaries: The absolute and relative growth rates are -0.279 and -0.339. This finding is consistent with the hypothesis that declines in acquired establishment employment are partly attributable to, and offset by, transfers, but it does not prove the hypothesis. The declines in employment might be greater in establishments acquired by multiple-auxiliary firms because the acquired establishment personnel to a greater extent duplicate the personnel already employed by the acquiring firm. The fact that more jobs are lost in these establishments does not necessarily mean that existing auxiliaries of acquiring firms are gaining jobs via transfer; the jobs might be eliminated altogether.

To shed light on this issue, we ran a regression similar to equation (1), also including a dummy variable equal to 1 if the 1982 owner of the establishment had acquired other auxiliary establishments since 1977, and otherwise equal to zero. The estimate (t-statistic) of the coefficient on this variable based on data for all industries was 0.007 (0.4), indicating that establishments owned by firms acquiring other establishments do not grow any faster than average. The estimate based on the subset of manufacturing establishments, however, was larger and significantly different from zero: 0.074 (2.8). Thus manufacturing auxiliaries owned by firms acquiring other auxiliaries tend to grow faster than average. But it seems likely that firms engaged in acquisition experience higher growth in nonauxiliary employment (via the construction and expansion of production facilities) than nonacquiring firms, so the higher growth in these establishments may not merely be offsetting declines in acquired auxiliaries.

The second approach we took to assess the issue of possible shifting of employees among auxiliaries was to construct firm-level data on auxiliary intensity and link them to establishment-level data. The auxiliary-intensity measure was constructed as follows. First, we aggregated the auxiliary establishment employment data (for all establishments, not just those present in both years) for 1977 and 1982 to the firm level using parent-

Table 4.7
Mean levels and changes in parent-firm's auxiliary intensity, by ownership-change status of auxiliary establishment

	Year		
	1977	1982	Change, 1977–82
(1) No ownership change	0.140	0.170	0.030
(2) Ownership change	0.148	0.044	−0.104
(3) Difference ((2) − (1))	0.008	−0.126	−0.133
	(1.9)	(27.0)	(46.3)
(4) Difference adjusted for industry effects	−0.002	−0.088	−0.086
	(0.6)	(18.5)	(24.8)

Note: t-statistics to test H_0: difference = 0 are in parentheses. $N = 5,538$.

company identification codes. For a nonrandom subset of almost 2,800 firms we were able to obtain data on total company employment from a third data source, the NSF/Census Survey of Industrial R&D. (The firms for which these data were available tend to be large, R&D-intensive manufacturing firms.) We then calculated for this subset of firms the ratio of auxiliary employment to total employment in both 1977 and 1982. This enabled us to determine for each of 5,538 surviving auxiliaries (out of 18,757 such auxiliaries) the auxiliary intensity of the establishment's parent firm in both 1977 and 1982. Mean values of the 1977 and 1982 ratios and of their difference (both unadjusted and adjusted for industry effects) by value of the ownership-change dummy OC, are reported in table 4.7. The parent firms of auxiliaries that changed owners between 1977 and 1982 were slightly more auxiliary intensive in 1977 than the parents of non-changers, although the adjusted difference is negative and insignificant. The auxiliary intensity of parents of auxiliaries that did not change owners increased from 14.0 to 17.0 percent, whereas that of auxiliaries that changed owners decreased 70 percent, from 17.8 to 4.4 percent. The unadjusted difference between change and no-change establishments in the growth of parent's auxiliary intensity is − 13.3 percent and highly significantly different from zero. Adjusting for industry effects reduces the magnitude of this difference by about a third, but it remains very large and significant.

Even the adjusted difference implies a percentage reduction in auxiliary-intensity associated with ownership change about six times as large as that estimated in the previous section. This procedure's estimate of the magnitude of the effect may be greater in part because to some extent it takes into account the opening and closing of auxiliaries, whereas the earlier procedure did not. Since establishments changing owners evidently have significantly lower employment growth, they are probably also more likely to close than nonchangers, and our previous estimates would not have captured this.

To summarize the analysis of this section, we have attempted to determine whether our estimate of the reduction in R associated with ownership change is biased due to transfers of employees among auxiliary establishments. Our first approach indicated that the acquiring firm does not own other auxiliaries in the case of three-fourths of auxiliary acquisitions, so no such transfers could occur. Even in these cases there were substantial declines in auxiliary employment. However, the declines were much greater among auxiliaries acquired by firms owning other auxiliaries. Thus, even though these constitute the minority of cases, they contribute importantly to the overall or average estimated effect of ownership change on auxiliary employment growth. These findings are consistent with the transfer hypothesis, which could imply that we have overestimated somewhat the reduction in R associated with ownership change, but they are consistent with other interpretations as well, which do not necessarily imply any overstatement.

The second approach, which examined the change in auxiliary intensity of the parent firm as a function of ownership-change status, suggested that we may have considerably underestimated the effect of ownership change on R, in part perhaps because of the censoring of auxiliaries that closed. Thus, although the possibility of overestimation due to transfers of employees cannot be entirely ruled out, there is much stronger evidence in support of the contrary position, that our estimates based on table 4.4 are conservative.

The Relationship between Firm Size and Administrative Intensity

Table 4.2 provided aggregate time-series data on the relationship between auxiliary-establishment employment and production-establishment employment. We believe that firm-level cross-sectional data characterizing this relationship are also of interest. A number of economists and organization theorists have developed theoretical models of the hierarchical or administrative structure of organizations. These models have testable implications for the relationship between the number of administrative employees A and the number of production employees P. Starbuck (1964, 499) observes that early organization theorists tended to view the administrative structure as a pyramidal hierarchy. One person comprises the top level in this hierarchy. He or she has S subordinates who comprise the second level; each of these has S subordinates, giving S^2 people in the third level, and so forth. (S is referred to as the "span of control.") The total number of administrators in a hierarchy with Θ levels is $A = (S^\Theta - 1)/(S - 1)$. If there are π production workers per foreman, then the total number of production workers is $P = \pi * S^{\Theta-1}$ and total employment is

$$T = A + P = \left(\frac{S^\Theta - 1}{S - 1}\right) + (\pi * S^{\Theta-1}).$$

Starbuck showed that, for plausible, assumed values of S and π, the ratio A/P would be essentially independent of T (or Θ) for values of T above a relatively low threshhold (i.e., $T = 100$). In other words, increasing the number Θ of hierarchical levels of an organization (hence its size T) would generally not result in an increase in the proportion of administrative employees.[17] Similarly Beckmann (1977, 1) argued that the claim that "increasing size of the organization burdens every productive worker with an ever increasing number of administrators per production worker" was not theoretically valid. Previous theorists, such as Knight and Kaldor, had hypothesized that there are increasing costs of administration per worker. In the presence of increasing returns to production activities (which they also hypothesized), the existence of an optimal firm size required there to be diseconomies of administration.

Existing evidence on the relationship across organizations between administrative intensity (A/P) and size (T) is very limited. Starbuck (1964, 501–502) cites four studies: one of California school districts, which found a positive relationship; two of firms, which found essentially no relationship; and one of 30 organizations of various kinds, which found a slightly negative relationship. We seek to shed further light on this relationship by examining the correlation across firms between total firm employment and (1) employment in auxiliary establishments, (2) nonproduction employment in production establishments, and (3) the sum of (1) and (2).

Perhaps the most straightforward way to examine the relationship between total firm employment and auxiliary employment would be to regress the logarithm of auxiliary-establishment employment on the logarithm of total employment. But 55 percent of the firms in our sample did not have any auxiliary establishments.[18] Therefore we decided to examine this relationship nonparametrically, by ranking and grouping the firms into six size classes on the basis of total employment and by computing the ratio of auxiliary establishment employment to total firm employment in each class. We computed weighted ratios (the ratio of class means) rather

Table 4.8
Mean ratios of auxiliary and nonproduction employment to total employment, by size of firm

Size class[a]	Mean total employment	Mean ratio to total employment of:		
		Auxiliary employment	Nonproduction employment	Auxiliary plus nonproduction employment
1	255	3.2%	30.8%	34.0%
2	608	4.9	29.4	34.3
3	1,148	7.2	29.1	36.3
4	2,309	8.9	32.1	41.0
5	6,170	10.7	26.6	37.3
6	34,213	12.3	29.4	41.8

a. Firms were ranked and grouped into six size classes on the basis of total employment. There are 276 or 277 firms in each size class.

than unweighted ratios (the class mean of the ratio) because the latter are more sensitive to outliers, particularly among the smallest size classes. The results are presented in table 4.8. The ratio of auxiliary employment to total employment is strictly increasing with respect to firm size. However, as noted above, nonproduction employees in production establishments might also be considered "administrators" (albeit ones lower down in the corporate hierarchy), and they outnumber auxiliary employees by about 4 to 1, so this positive relationship is not necessarily inconsistent with the pyramidal model of organization sketched above. It is possible that larger firms merely tend to centralize administrators in auxiliary establishments, that is, to substitute auxiliary employees for nonproduction employees in production establishments. The last two columns of table 4.8 do not support this view, however. The penultimate column displays the estimated ratios of NP employment to total employment.[19] The relationship between total employment and the employment share of NP workers is fairly noisy, but it appears to have a slope of zero. The sum of the two employment shares is shown in the last column. While a positive relationship is far less clear than it is in the third column, such a relationship appears to exist: Swapping the ratios for groups 4 and 5 yields a monotonic relationship, and the combined mean of the first three groups is 0.349, while that of the last three groups is 0.400.

In conclusion, large firms employ a higher fraction of their employees in auxiliary establishments, and they don't appear to employ a smaller fraction of employees as nonproduction workers in production establishments.

Hence contrary to the implications of a certain class of hierarchical models of the firm, there seem to exist diseconomies of administration.

Summary and Conclusions

In this chapter we have reported analyses of three large Census Bureau establishment- or firm-level data sets designed to yield insight into the effect of changes in ownership on the employment and wages of several important categories of workers. We were particularly concerned with the effects on workers in auxiliary establishments, since it is there that top managers and administrators and many R&D personnel are employed. Since the number of these (relatively highly paid) workers is small compared to the number in production establishments, the effects of ownership change on them have not been captured or have been heavily masked in previous studies of the labor impact of takeovers.

One of our major findings is that employment growth is much lower —17 percentage points lower over five years—in auxiliary establishments changing owners than in those not changing owners. Mean employment growth is slightly positive for establishments not changing owners and is sharply negative for establishments changing owners. There is, however, no significant difference between changers and nonchangers in the growth of R&D employment.

The increase in payroll per employee was 9 percentage points lower among auxiliary establishments changing owners than it was among other auxiliary establishments, controlling for industry and the initial wage rate. The relative decline in total compensation (including supplements to payroll) was perhaps one-third higher, about 12 percentage points.

The relative declines in employment and wages of workers in auxiliary establishments are about three times as great as the corresponding declines in production establishments. In the latter case the data indicate that the declines occur immediately before ownership change and are to a small extent reversed soon after. Unfortunately, due to the low frequency of the auxiliary establishment data, we cannot determine how much of the employment and wage declines there occurred before rather than after ownership change. Even if the declines occurred prior to ownership change, it is evident that the new owners chose not to restore the employment and wage cuts. This implies that ownership change results in reductions in the wage and especially in the employment of auxiliary-establishment employees relative to those of production-establishment employees. Taken at face value, it implies that the ratio of auxiliary-establishment to production-establishment employment declines 11.2 percent in firms involved in ownership change relative to firms not so involved. This translates into the elimination of 7.2 auxiliary-establishment jobs for every 1,000 production-establishment jobs. It is possible that due to transfers of employees between auxiliaries, this figure is an overestimate. But one attempt to account for employment in nonacquired establishments of acquiring firms provided much stronger evidence for the proposition that this estimate is too conservative.

Some people express concern about the number of lawyers, investment bankers, and other highly paid professionals devoted to facilitating or implementing takeovers, and claim that this may constitute a waste of valuable human resources. But the quantity and quality of labor engaged in this activity may not be high relative to the quantity and quality of central-office labor "saved" as a consequence of ownership change.

Because we failed to account for auxiliary-establishment employment in our earlier investigation of the effects of ownership change on productivity, we appear to have underestimated the productivity gain associated with ownership change by about 75 percent.

In addition to revealing important differences between the effects of ownership change on auxiliary and production establishments, our analysis also indicated clear (although smaller) differences between its effects on production and nonproduction workers in production establishments. Only the production employees in these establishments appear to experience relative employment declines in connection with changes in ownership. Because the relative employment of nonproduction employees in production establishments does not decline, the overall ratio of indirect to direct labor is not reduced in the course of ownership change. But the composition or locus of indirect labor does change significantly, as the fraction of it accounted for by auxiliary establishments is reduced.

The chapter also provided some evidence concerning the relationship between firm size and administrative intensity. Certain models of organizational structure imply that administrative intensity should be constant or even declining with respect to firm size throughout most of the range of firm size, but our data failed to support this hypothesis. The ratio of auxiliary employment to total employment appears to be strictly increasing with respect to firm size, whereas the ratio of other indirect labor to total employment appears to be independent of firm size.

5   Leveraged Buyouts

with Donald Siegel

This chapter investigates the effects of leveraged buyouts on total-factor productivity and related aspects of firm behavior. In an LBO a group of investors (which sometimes includes incumbent management) takes a company (or a division of a company) private by purchasing all of the outstanding equity of the company, mainly using borrowed funds. The enterprise is much more highly leveraged (it has a higher debt/equity ratio) after the LBO than before. The financing of LBOs often involves the sale of high-yield (or junk) bonds. The debt incurred to buy out the company is expected to be serviced by a combination of operating income and asset sales.

Although the LBO transaction has been in existence for at least 20 years, only in the 1980s has it become a quantitatively significant component of overall merger and acquisition (M&A) activity. The share of LBOs in the aggregate value of M&A transactions increased from almost zero in the 1970s to 27 percent in 1986. This increase is probably attributable to an important extent to the invention and diffusion of junk bond financing beginning in the late 1970s. Because the extent of LBO activity was negligible prior to about 1981, our analysis will focus primarily on the period 1981–86.

The transition from a diffusely owned, publicly held corporation to an LBO partnership generally involves a number of significant changes in the structure and governance of the enterprise. First, the increase in leverage sharply increases the firm's fixed-interest obligations. If managers fail to meet these obligations, they risk losing control of the firm to creditors. Second, equity ownership by management tends to increase. Jensen and Murphy (1990, table 3) state that the median CEO in a sample of LBO organizations has a 6.4 percent equity interest, whereas the median CEO in a Forbes 1000 firm has a 0.2 percent interest. Kaplan (1989) and Smith (1990) estimate that median postbuyout equity ownership by (all) management is 22.6 and 16.7 percent, respectively, far higher than in public companies. Third, almost half of all LBOs are of divisions rather than entire firms, so postbuyout firms are often less hierarchical and more focused than the companies from which they emerged. Jensen notes that the typical corporate headquarters staff of hundreds or thousands is replaced by an LBO association staff numbering in the tens. Other organizational changes that may result from leveraged transactions are a modified relation between managers and the board of directors and the introduction of debt-covenant-imposed constraints on managers (Baker and Wruck 1989).

Since many of the changes in incentives and control align managers' interests with those of the firm's shareholders, it is hypothesized that LBOs result in improvements in companies' operating performance. Several studies using firm-level data have analyzed the effect of LBOs on various indicators of postbuyout performance. Some have examined a fairly indirect (ex ante) measure of performance: the equity premium associated with the transaction. (See Amihud 1989 for a survey of the evidence on equity premiums.) Others (Kaplan 1989; Smith 1990; Baker and Wruck 1989) have analyzed direct (ex post) measures, such as operating earnings and net cash flows.

The objective of this chapter is also to investigate the effect of LBOs on operating performance, but we use a different ex post measure of performance and a new data base at a lower level of aggregation: the plant level. The performance measure we use is total-factor productivity (TFP), or output per unit of total input. Theoretical models developed by Baily and Schultze (1990) and by Allen, Faulhaber, and MacKinlay (1989) imply that productivity is positively correlated with both profitability and stock prices but that productivity is more fundamental: It determines the other two variables.[1]

Our data base is an extract from the U.S. Census Bureau's Longitudinal Research Database (LRD) described in chapter 2 and linked to a list of LBOs provided by Morgan Stanley and Co. The LRD extract contains annual data on output, capital, labor, materials, plant closings, wages, and other variables for over 20,000 manufacturing establishments in the years 1972–86. The LRD offers a number of important advantages for examining the effects of LBOs on performance. Unlike publicly available data sources, it includes observations on privately as well as publicly owned firms. By definition, firms that have undergone an LBO are (at least initially) privately held and are therefore not generally required by the Securities and Exchange Commission to issue financial data. Firms offering common stock or with public debt or preferred stock outstanding after a buyout issue such data, but these may be a nonrandom sample of all firms involved in LBOs.

As a plant-level data base the LRD has additional advantages. Almost half of major LBOs have been of divisions rather than entire firms. Studies such as Kaplan (1989) and Smith (1990) have had to confine their attention to buyouts of firms because data at the divisional or lower level are not generally publicly available, even for publicly held companies. The LRD permits us to analyze partial-firm as well as full-firm LBOs. Moreover LBOs are frequently followed by divestiture of some of the firm's plants or lines of business, further limiting the usefulness of company-level data.

Several other methodological advantages of our data are worth noting. We examine the impact of both LBOs in general and management buyouts in particular. We have wage as well as employment data for both nonproduction (white-collar) and production (blue-collar) workers in manufacturing establishments.

Despite these advantages our study is subject to a number of limitations. First, we can determine whether LBOs are accompanied by changes in the relative productivity of the plants involved, but we cannot establish whether LBOs cause these changes. Suppose we find that plants involved in management buyouts in year t experience greater improvements in productivity between $t - 1$ and $t + 3$ than plants not involved in buyouts. It is possible that the relative productivity increase would have occurred in the absence of buyouts and that the buyout occurred because managers had private advance information about the increase. We cannot rule out this interpretation of a pre- versus postbuyout productivity increase, but Kaplan (1989) and Smith (1990) have presented several kinds of evidence that do not support it.

Second, LBOs might be postulated to result in increases in the firm's owners' risks (e.g., of bankruptcy) as well as in their returns. Indeed the increase in risk, or in the sensitivity of financial rewards to company performance, is posited to be partly responsible for the increase in returns. We attempt to measure the increase in mean returns (productivity) associated with buyouts, but we cannot measure the increase in financial risk.

Third, the LRD does not include a number of important variables, such as output and materials prices. It covers only the manufacturing sector and does not include data for administrative offices (corporate headquarters) and other auxiliary establishments. These omissions make it difficult for us to rule out alternative interpretations of our results.

All of the buyouts in our sample occurred in 1981 or later, and 1986 is the latest year for which census data were available, so we can provide productivity estimates for four or five postbuyout years for transactions occurring in 1981 or 1982. This is a longer period than those in other studies, some of which analyzed data for only the first year following the buyout. Because LBOs before 1983 were few and small, however, our estimates after the third postbuyout year ($t + 3$) are much less precise than those up to three years after the buyout. Also we provide evidence that the impact of pre-1983 buyouts on productivity in years $t + 1$ to $t + 3$ was different from the corresponding impact of later buyouts. Thus our estimates for years $t + 4$ and $t + 5$ (based only on early buyouts) may be poor indicators of the longer-term effects of later buyouts.

Identification of Plants Involved in LBO

To measure the effect of LBOs on the relative efficiency of plants, we need to determine which LRD plants were involved in LBOs and in what years. The LRD contains information on plant ownership change in general, but not on LBOs in particular. We therefore obtained from Morgan Stanley & Co. a list of LBOs that occurred from 1979 through 1988 and linked this list to our extract of the LRD. Morgan Stanley compiles a data base on all major mergers and acquisitions of which LBOs are a subset. The primary sources from which the data base is compiled are reports in *The New York Times*, the *Wall Street Journal*, Dow Jones tapes, and news releases. Transactions are identified as LBOs in the Morgan Stanley data base if they are reported as such in the primary sources.

Only LBOs whose value is at least $35 million ("major LBOs") are included in the Morgan Stanley data base. The bottom panel of table 5.1 presents data for this subset of deals. In principle, of course, the total value of major LBOs cannot exceed the total value of all LBOs, but the data for the two groups come from different sources that in some cases assign different values to a given deal, so this inequality is sometimes violated in practice. Nevertheless, comparison of the top and bottom panels of the table provides a rough guide to the effect of the $35 million threshold. For the period as a whole, major LBOs account for 19 percent of the deals but 96 percent of the total value. Since the same nominal threshhold is in effect in every year, the fraction of deals exceeding the threshhold tends to be larger toward the end of the period.

The establishment records in the LRD indicate both a code identifying the parent company and the (four-digit SIC) industry in which the establishment primarily operates. To determine whether an establishment was involved in an LBO in a given year, we look to see whether the parent

Table 5.1
Aggregate value and number of leveraged buyouts and mergers and acquisitions, 1981–86

Year	Leveraged buyouts			Mergers and acquisitions		
	Total value	Number	Average value	Total value	Number	Average value
Deals of all sizes						
1981	$3,093	99	$31.2	$82,600	2,395	$34.5
1982	3,452	164	21.0	53,700	2,346	22.9
1983	4,520	231	19.6	73,000	2,533	28.8
1984	18,810	253	74.3	122,300	2,543	48.1
1985	18,030	254	71.0	179,700	3,001	59.9
1986	46,620	333	140.0	173,100	3,336	51.9
Deals of value > $35 million						
1981	3,136	17	184.5	71,128	235	302.7
1982	3,422	21	162.9	47,836	246	194.5
1983	3,853	30	128.4	63,532	306	207.6
1984	18,805	53	354.8	121,274	403	300.9
1985	13,036	44	296.3	186,009	505	368.3
1986	43,850	79	555.1	198,190	768	258.1

Sources: Deals of all sizes: LBOs from *Mergers and Acquisitions*; M&As from W. T. Grimm & Co. Deals of value > $35 million: From Morgan Stanley and Co. data base.
Note: Values are in millions of dollars.

company's name appears on the list of companies acquired through LBOs in that year. If not, we assign the code LBO = 0 (not involved in an LBO in that year). If the name does appear, we determine whether the LBO was of the entire company or only a part. If the entire firm was bought out, we assign the code LBO = 1 (involved in an LBO in that year). If only part of the company was bought out, we determine the business it is in by comparing a business description of the unit contained in the Morgan Stanley data base with a list of SIC industries. Additional information about the industrial activities of divisions or companies is obtained from *Standard and Poor's Registry of Corporations* and the *Directory of Corporate Affiliations*. If the establishment's SIC code is included in this list, we assign the code LBO = 1; otherwise, we assign the code LBO = 0.

Roach (1989, 24) estimates that 63 percent of the value of the major LBOs during the period 1978–88 involved companies or divisions whose primary industry is manufacturing. Since only manufacturing establishments are included in the LRD, if the sizes of LBOs in manufacturing and other sectors are similar, one would expect to identify establishments in the

Table 5.2
Cumulative value and number of 1981–86 leveraged buyouts involving companies observed in Census Bureau's Longitudinal Research Database (LRD) extract, by selected attributes

	Total value	Number	Average value
Acquirers include management	$13,220	48	$275.4
Acquirers exclude management	35,715	83	430.3
LBO of entire firm	35,949	80	449.4
LBO of part of firm	12,992	51	254.7
All LBOs	48,941	131	373.6

Source: Morgan Stanley and Co. list of all LBOs during 1979–88 whose value exceeds $35 million, linked to an extract of the Census Bureau's Longitudinal Research Database containing annual data for 1972–86 on 20,493 manufacturing plants.
Note: Values are in millions of dollars.

LRD corresponding to no more than about 60 percent of the number or value of LBOs. We observe one or more establishments of companies involved in 57 percent by value of the major LBOs. Thus within the constraints of the deal-size threshhold and the industry limitation, the LRD's coverage appears to be good.

Kaplan (1989) and Smith (1990) have been concerned with management buyouts (MBOs), the subset of LBOs in which the acquirer includes the incumbent managers of the acquired unit. Since the description of the acquirer indicates whether management participated in the acquisition, we can distinguish between MBOs and other LBOs. As table 5.2 reveals, MBOs accounted for 27 percent of the total value of major LBOs involving companies included in our extract of the LRD. (MBOs account for 45 percent of the value of all major LBOs during the period 1981–86.)

Our extract from the LRD contains data on 20,493 manufacturing establishments for 1981. Eleven hundred and eight (5.4 percent) of these establishments were involved in a major LBO during the period 1981–86. (Our LRD extract does not include any establishments owned by firms involved in the few 1979 and 1980 deals shown on the Morgan Stanley list.) The distribution of establishments involved in major LBOs (henceforth "LBO establishments"), by type of LBO, is presented in table 5.3. Thirty-five percent of the LBO establishments are involved in MBOs, and 30 percent are involved in partial-firm LBOs. These two attributes are correlated: MBOs account for 47 percent of partial-firm LBOs but only 30 percent of full-firm LBOs.

Table 5.3
Distribution of LRD establishments involved in major LBOs during 1981–86

	MBOs	Other LBOs	Total
Full-firm LBOs	239	553	791
Partial-firm LBOs	160	180	340
Total	399	733	1,132

Source: Morgan Stanley and Co. list of all LBOs during 1979–88 whose value exceeds $35 million, linked to an extract of the Census Bureau's Longitudinal Research Database containing annual data for 1972–86 on 20,493 manufacturing plants.
Note: Sums do not exactly match because several plants were involved in more than one type of transaction.

Econometric Issues in Estimating Productivity Differences between LBO and non-LBO Plants

We seek to obtain consistent and efficient estimates of the difference in productivity between LBO and non-LBO plants in the years before and after the buyout and to test the null hypothesis that the pre- versus postbuyout change in this difference is zero. We can measure the mean productivity differences by estimating a set of equations

$$e_{i,t+k} = \Theta_k BO_{i,t} + w_{i,t+k},\tag{1}$$

where $e_{i,t+k}$ is the productivity residual of plant i in year $t + k$ ($k = -8, -7, \ldots, 4, 5$), $BO_{i,t}$ equals either $LBO_{i,t}$ (equal to 1 if plant i was involved in any leveraged buyout in year t; otherwise, equal to zero) or $MBO_{i,t}$ (equal to 1 if plant i was involved in a management buyout in year t; otherwise, equal to zero), w is a disturbance term, and the intercept is suppressed for simplicity. The parameter Θ_k is the difference in (population) mean productivity in year $t + k$ between plants involved and not involved in buyouts in year t. For example, if $BO = $ MBO, $t = 1983$, and $k = 2$, Θ_k is the difference in 1985 productivity between plants involved in 1983 MBOs and those not involved. The set of equations (1) is estimated as a system. So to test the hypothesis of no change in the mean productivity difference from, say, 1 year before to k years after the buyout, we can test the significance of $(\Theta_k - \Theta_{-1})$.

Several econometric issues concerning (1) should be noted. First, the dependent variable e, hence the disturbance w, of the equation is heteroskedastic, but estimation of the first-stage equation provides us with consistent estimates of $\mathrm{var}(e_{i,t+k})$. We therefore estimate this equation with weighted-least-squares, with weights equal to $[\mathrm{var}(e_{i,t+k})]^{-1/2}$.

Second, our procedure for assigning values to the buyout codes $LBO_{i,t}$ and $MBO_{i,t}$ is undoubtedly subject to error, particularly for partial-firm buyouts. For example, if two subsidiaries of a firm both have plants in the same industry, and only one subsidiary is involved in a buyout, we would erroneously assign the value $LBO = 1$ to both subsidiaries' establishments. If, however, such measurement errors are random (as we expect), their effect will be to bias the point estimates and t-statistics of the Θ_k toward zero.

Third, because our sample is truncated in 1986 and over two-thirds of the sample plants ever involved in LBOs were involved in them in 1984 or later, the precision of our estimates of Θ_k, and the power of our tests concerning them, decline as k increases from 1 to 5, particularly when k increases above 3. (The variance of the estimates of Θ_k is inversely related to the number of plants observed k years after a buyout.) The decline in precision is especially pronounced for management buyouts, since the number of plants involved in MBOs increased faster during the 1981–86 period than the number involved in all LBOs.

In principle one could estimate a separate set of equations for each of the six years ($t = 1981, \ldots, 1986$) in which buyouts occurred in our sample. If the buyouts that occurred in different years had similar effects on productivity, however, pooling the data for the various buyout cohorts will substantially improve the efficiency of our estimates. (It will also greatly reduce the number of estimates.) Our initial estimates are based on a pooled sample.[2] We subsequently explore whether these estimates mask important differences between the productivity effects of different buyout cohorts.

We estimate the difference between the median, as well as the mean, productivity of buyout and nonbuyout plants. If productivity is normally distributed, the sample mean is a more efficient estimator of the population's central tendency than the sample median.[3] (Also it is simpler to perform hypothesis tests on linear combinations [averages or differences] of parameters using means than using medians.) On the other hand, the median is a more robust estimator: It is less sensitive to outliers, and, more generally, to departures from normality.

Estimates of the Productivity Equations

Differences between the mean and median levels of productivity of buyout and nonbuyout plants are reported in table 5.4. The differences between the means are estimates of the parameters Θ_k from equation (1) and are

Table 5.4
Differences (in percent) between the mean and median productivity in year $t + k$
($k = -8, -7, \ldots, 4, 5$) of plants involved in buyouts in year t and those not involved

Year	Difference in mean (t-statistic) LBO (1)	MBO (2)	Difference in median (significance level) LBO (3)	MBO (4)	Number of plants LBO (5)	MBO (6)
$t - 8$	1.2 (1.5)	0.2 (0.1)	1.4 (0.29)	1.0 (0.46)	983	366
$t - 7$	1.0 (1.4)	2.0 (1.6)	0.6 (0.46)	2.2 (0.05)	983	366
$t - 6$	0.9 (1.2)	-0.4 (-0.3)	0.7 (0.45)	0.4 (0.48)	983	366
$t - 5$	1.6 (2.6)	0.9 (0.9)	1.3 (0.30)	1.4 (0.24)	983	366
$t - 4$	1.7 (2.4)	0.2 (0.2)	0.7 (0.42)	0.1 (0.54)	983	366
$t - 3$	1.7 (2.6)	2.3 (1.9)	2.0 (0.07)	2.3 (0.04)	983	366
$t - 2$	1.9 (2.4)	3.4 (2.9)	2.2 (0.05)	3.3 (0.03)	983	366
$t - 1$	1.5 (1.8)	7.2 (4.3)	2.6 (0.03)	4.1 (0.02)	983	366
t	2.7 (2.7)	4.9 (2.9)	3.3 (0.03)	3.4 (0.03)	983	366
$t + 1$	4.5 (3.5)	9.4 (4.1)	6.7 (0.02)	7.9 (0.02)	636	236
$t + 2$	3.1 (2.0)	11.4 (4.0)	4.2 (0.03)	6.6 (0.02)	481	183
$t + 3$	4.1 (1.9)	9.9 (3.1)	6.9 (0.02)	4.7 (0.03)	245	114
$t + 4$	-3.8 (-1.3)	-2.9 (-0.5)	-2.8 (0.25)	-4.3 (0.09)	136	22
$t + 5$	5.6 (1.4)	-15.8 (-1.4)	6.1 (0.15)	-14.4 (0.17)	59	10

Note: The sample is an extract of the Census Bureau's Longitudinal Research Database linked to Morgan Stanley data on LBOs and includes annual data for the years 1972–86 on 12,895 continuously observed manufacturing plants. The mean productivity differences are estimates of the parameter θ_k from the equation $e_{i,t+k} = \Theta_k BO_{i,t} + w_{i,t+k}$, where $e_{i,t+k}$ is the productivity residual of plant i in year $t + k$; $BO_{i,t}$ is defined either as $LBO_{i,t}$ (equal to 1 if plant i was involved in any leveraged buyout in year t and otherwise equal to zero) or as $MBO_{i,t}$ (equal to 1 if plant i was involved in a management buyout in year t and otherwise equal to zero), and w is a disturbance. The equations are estimated by weighted least squares, with consistent estimates of $[\text{var}(e_{i,t+k})]^{-1/2}$ as weights. The reported means are the Θ_k multiplied by 100 and therefore represent percentage differences in mean productivity. The significance level for the difference in median is the probability value from the Kruskal-Wallis test.

displayed in columns 1 and 2. We consider first the estimates corresponding to all LBOs, shown in column 1. All of the coefficients corresponding
to the prebuyout years $(\Theta_{-8}, \ldots, \Theta_{-1})$ are positive, indicating that plants
involved in buyouts were more efficient than nonbuyout plants in the years
before the buyout. The coefficients Θ_{-8}, Θ_{-7}, and Θ_{-6} are not significantly different from zero, however, whereas the coefficients Θ_{-5} to Θ_{-1}
are significant and larger. Plants involved in buyouts in year t are 1.5 to 1.9
percent more efficient during $t - 5$ to $t - 1$ than plants not involved in
buyouts in year t.

The difference between the mean productivity of buyout and nonbuyout
plants is larger in the first three years after the buyout than in any of the
eight years before the buyout, ranging from 3.1 to 4.5 percent. The difference, $\Theta_A - \Theta_B$, between the average of the first three coefficients after the
buyout, $\Theta_A \equiv (\Theta_1 + \Theta_2 + \Theta_3)/3$, and the average of the first three before the buyout, $\Theta_B \equiv (\Theta_{-1} + \Theta_{-2} + \Theta_{-3})/3$, is 2.2, significant at the
0.02 level (t-statistic $= 2.3$). This finding is consistent with the hypothesis
that buyouts are associated with increases in productivity, at least in the
short run (the first three years after the buyout).

The coefficients for years $t + 4$ and $t + 5$ are both insignificant, however, and the $t + 4$ coefficient is negative. In principle it is possible that the
lower values of Θ_4 and Θ_5 are attributable to a few extreme observations,
especially because these estimates are based on a much smaller number of
buyouts. The difference between the median productivity of buyout and
nonbuyout plants exhibits the same basic time profile, however, as the
difference between means. The differences between medians are positive in
all eight years $t - 8$ to $t - 1$ but are significant only in $t - 3$ to $t - 1$,
where they range from 2.0 to 2.6 percent. The differences in medians are
substantially larger in the first three postbuyout years, averaging 5.9 percent. The differences between medians, like the differences between means,
are insignificant in years $t + 4$ and $t + 5$.

Below we enumerate several possible explanations for the finding that
Θ_4 and Θ_5 are smaller and/or less significant than Θ_1 to Θ_3 and attempt
to determine which explanation is correct. But first we examine the coeffi-
cients corresponding to management buyouts. The differences between
means, shown in column 3, are in some ways similar to the estimates for all
LBOs. The $t - 8$ to $t - 4$ differences are insignificant, whereas those for
$t - 3$ to $t - 1$ are positive and significant. Moreover the latter coefficients
are larger than their all-LBO counterparts and show a marked positive
trend. The relative efficiency of MBO plants was increasing, as well as
positive, in the three years preceeding the buyout.

The mean and median MBO productivity differentials are larger in each of the three years after the buyout than in the three years before. The mean (median) values of Θ_A, Θ_B, and $\Theta_A - \Theta_B$ are 10.2 (6.4), 4.3 (3.2), and 5.9 (3.2). Thus the mean estimates suggest that MBOs are associated with greater short-run productivity increases than LBOs, but the median estimates imply that the productivity increases for MBOs are about the same as those for all LBOs. As with all LBOs, both mean and median estimates are insignificant in years $t + 4$ and $t + 5$; moreover all four of these estimates are negative.

There are two possible explanations for the finding that the coefficients for years $t + 1$ to $t + 3$ are significantly greater than the coefficients for $t - 3$ to $t - 1$, whereas the coefficients for $t + 4$ and $t + 5$ are not. The first is that LBOs have a merely transitory positive impact on TFP, which vanishes, and after three years perhaps even becomes negative.

Several theoretical arguments could be made to support that hypothesis. First, it is possible that, after an LBO, resources that were previously allocated to producing long-term intangible investment goods such as R&D capital and customer goodwill are shifted to producing current output. This would result in a temporary surge in measured productivity followed by a gradual decline as the stocks of intangible capital were depleted. Alternatively, one might hypothesize that a radical change in organizational form has a high initial impact on productivity due to its shock value but that the effect decays or depreciates as managers and workers become accustomed to the new form.

Finally, asset sales could contribute to a decline in the mean and median productivity of plants that have undergone LBOs. Bhagat, Shleifer, and Vishny (1990) report that an unweighted average of 44 percent of assets acquired in LBOs during 1984–86 were sold (primarily to public companies) by the end of the third year following the LBO. It is conceivable that the productivity of plants remaining within the LBO organizational form increases permanently but that the sale of plants to public companies reduces their productivity (perhaps to prebuyout levels).[4] In this case, the average productivity of plants involved in buyouts would decline over time, as the fraction of plants remaining within the LBO form decreased.

But the finding that the productivity estimates for $t + 1$ to $t + 3$ are positive, significant, and relatively large, whereas those for $t + 4$ and $t + 5$ are insignificant and often negative could also be an artifact of pooling the data across calendar years. Since the census data do not extend past 1986, the $t + 4$ and $t + 5$ estimates are based only on buyouts occurring in 1981 and 1982 (henceforth referred to as *early* buyouts), whereas the $t + 1$ to

$t + 3$ estimates are also based on *later* buyouts. The contrast between the
two sets of estimates may be due to differences between the productivity
effect of early and later buyouts, rather than to the tendency of productivity to decline after a typical buyout. As demographers would say, our
estimates may reflect cohort effects rather than age effects.

To investigate this possibility, we estimate a modified version of (1) in
which the dummy variable BO is replaced by two dummies, BO^E ($= 1$ if the
plant was involved in an early buyout; otherwise, equal to zero) and BO^L
($= 1$ if the plant was involved in a later [1983–86] buyout; otherwise, equal
to zero). The estimates for all LBOs are presented in columns 1 and 2 of
table 5.5. They are consistent with the hypothesis that only the later
buyouts had a significant positive effect on productivity during years $t + 1$
to $t + 3$. The early LBO coefficients for $t + 1$ to $t + 3$ are insignificant and
smaller than the corresponding coefficients for later LBOs. The LBOs that
occurred in 1981 and 1982 apparently did not have a significant effect on
productivity in any postbuyout year. In sharp contrast, 1983–86 LBOs had
an impact in years $t + 1$ to $t + 3$ even greater than that implied by the
pooled estimates in table 5.4 (the latter are essentially weighted averages
of the early and late LBO coefficients). The late LBO coefficients also show
an upward trend after the buyout: The $t + 3$ coefficient is about twice as
large as the $t + 1$ and $t + 2$ coefficients.

With management buyouts the contrast between early and late buyout
effects is somewhat different. (These estimates are much less precise than
those for all LBOs because of both the smaller number of MBO plants and
the smaller proportion of early MBOs.) Early MBOs apparently had a
strong positive impact on productivity in $t + 1$. Indeed, it was stronger
than the $t + 1$ impact of later MBOs. But the early MBO impact is insignificant and/or negative, and it tends to decline in years $t + 2$ to $t + 5$.
On the other hand, the impact of late MBOs is positive, significant, and
increasing from $t + 1$ to $t + 3$.

The estimates disaggregated by cohort (early versus late) suggest that
the decline in the pooled coefficients after $t + 3$ is due almost entirely to
cohort effects (differences between the productivity effects of early and late
buyouts) rather than to age effects (depreciation of the impact of a typical
buyout). Only among early MBOs, which accounted for just 28 (3 percent)
of the 983 plants involved in all buyouts in our sample, is there any
evidence of such depreciation. The estimates corresponding to all early
LBOs suggest zero depreciation, and those corresponding to later buyouts
(both all LBOs and MBOs) suggest that the productivity impact can increase from $t + 1$ to $t + 3$. We cannot determine whether the productivity

Table 5.5
Productivity effects (in percent) of early (1981–82) and late (1983–86) buyouts

Year	Early LBO (1)	Late LBO (2)	Early MBO (3)	Late MBO (4)	Number of plants early/late LBO (5)	MBO (6)
$t - 8$	−1.8	2.5%	0.2%	1.0%	204/779	28/338
	(−0.9)	(2.9)	(0.1)	(0.1)		
$t - 7$	2.3	2.3	0.9	2.4	204/779	28/338
	(1.1)	(2.7)	(0.2)	(1.8)		
$t - 6$	1.0	1.4	−0.6	0.2	204/779	28/338
	(0.8)	(1.7)	(−0.1)	(0.1)		
$t - 5$	2.4	1.6	0.6	1.1	204/779	28/338
	(1.3)	(2.5)	(1.1)	(1.1)		
$t - 4$	1.9	1.8	−0.1	0.5	204/779	28/338
	(1.1)	(2.5)	(−0.0)	(0.4)		
$t - 3$	2.6	1.8	5.0	2.4	204/779	28/338
	(1.4)	(2.6)	(0.9)	(1.9)		
$t - 2$	0.1	1.5	4.3	3.1	204/779	28/338
	(0.6)	(1.6)	(0.8)	(2.3)		
$t - 1$	1.2	2.7	5.4	6.9	204/779	28/338
	(1.0)	(2.2)	(1.5)	(3.7)		
t	2.4	2.9	7.1	3.8	204/779	28/338
	(1.5)	(2.4)	(1.6)	(2.0)		
$t + 1$	3.4	6.0	16.6	8.2	190/446	26/210
	(1.2)	(4.0)	(2.1)	(3.4)		
$t + 2$	−4.9	6.4	4.8	9.9	160/321	25/158
	(−1.6)	(3.4)	(0.7)	(3.7)		
$t + 3$	−3.0	12.4	3.4	13.5	142/103	24/90
	(−1.0)	(3.8)	(0.4)	(3.6)		
$t + 4$	−3.8	—	−2.9	—	136/0	22/0
	(−1.3)		(−0.5)			
$t + 5$	5.6	—	−15.8	—	59/0	10/0
	(1.4)		(−1.4)			

Note: The sample is an extract of the Census Bureau's Longitudinal Research Database linked to Morgan Stanley data on LBOs and includes annual data for 1972–86 on 12,895 continuously observed manufacturing plants. Differences between the mean productivity in year $t + k$ ($k = -8, -7, \ldots, 4, 5$) of plants involved in buyouts in year t and those not involved (t-statistics in parentheses). The mean productivity differences are estimates of the parameters Θ_k^E and Θ_k^L from the equation

$$e_{i,t+k} = \Theta_k^E BO_{i,t}^E + \Theta_k^L BO_{i,t}^L + w_{i,t+k},$$

where $e_{i,t+k}$ is the productivity residual of plant i in year $t + k$, $BO_{i,t}^E$ is equal to 1 if plant i was involved in a buyout in year t ($t = 1981, 1982$) and is otherwise equal to zero; $BO_{i,t}^L$ is equal to 1 if plant i was involved in an buyout in year t ($t = 1983, \ldots, 1986$) and is otherwise equal to zero, and w is a disturbance. The equations are estimated by weighted least squares, with consistent estimates of $[\text{var}(e_{i,t+k})]^{-1/2}$ as weights. The tabulated figures are the estimates of Θ_k^E and Θ_k^L multiplied by 100 and therefore represent percentage differences in mean productivity.

impact of the 1983–86 buyouts persisted and/or continued to increase beyond $t + 3$ until we can obtain and analyze data for the post-1986 period.

The estimates suggest that later buyouts had a much more positive and significant impact on productivity than earlier buyouts. For all LBOs this is partly because MBOs are a higher proportion in the later period (43 versus 14 percent), and productivity increases more for MBOs than for all LBOs. However, table 5.5 indicates that (except in year $t + 1$) late MBOs have a larger impact than early MBOs, so not all of the early versus late LBO differential is explained by the increase in the relative importance of MBOs.

As noted earlier, some of the plants present in our sample in 1981 had closed by 1986, but the mean and median productivity estimates reported in tables 5.4 and 5.5 are based only on observations of continuously operating plants. Therefore these tables show that plants that were involved in buyouts in year t and remained in operation until at least $t + k$ ($k = 1, 2, 3$) showed greater productivity increases from $t - 1$ to $t + k$ than nonbuyout plants that survived until $t + k$. This finding could be partly or entirely an artifact of different survival (or plant closing) rates for buyout and nonbuyout plants. Consider the following set of assumptions: (1) Buyouts have no effect on the productivity of individual plants, (2) the proportion of plants closed between $t - 1$ and $t + k$ is higher for buyout than nonbuyout plants, and (3) within both groups the least efficient plants are closed.[5] Under these assumptions the difference between the mean or median productivity of buyout and nonbuyout plants would increase from $t - 1$ to $t + k$, even though buyouts do not affect the productivity of any individual plant because of different rates of attrition in the two populations.

To determine whether the mean and median productivity differences in tables 5.4 and 5.5 overstate the effects of buyouts on individual plants because of a higher closure rate among buyout plants, we calculate rates of survival from $t - 1$ to $t + k$ for both populations. The differences between the survival rates are not significantly different from zero. Also the point estimates of survival rates are slightly higher for buyout plants than for nonbuyout plants. Hence assumption 2 does not hold, and our estimates do not appear to be biased upward by different attrition rates.

Substitution of Compensation for Direct Monitoring of Production Workers

Jensen (1989) argues that one way LBO associations achieve efficiencies is by substituting incentives and compensation for direct monitoring by large bureaucratic staffs. The idea that a principal can elicit effort from his agents by compensation rather than monitoring has been developed in, among other places, the literature on efficiency wages (e.g., see Akerlof and Yellen 1986).

Although Jensen is referring primarily to senior and middle managers (who are often employed in auxiliary establishments and therefore not included in our sample), the substitution of compensation for monitoring could also apply to production workers. About 30 percent of the workers employed in manufacturing establishments are nonproduction workers, some of whom are supervisory employees above the working-supervisor level. If LBOs entail the substitution of compensation for direct monitoring of production workers by supervisors, one would expect to observe two pre- versus postbuyout changes: (1) a reduction in the ratio of nonproduction to production employment (or wage bill) and (2) an increase in the compensation of production workers.

Since the LRD includes employment and payroll data by category of worker (production versus nonproduction), we can test these hypotheses and, more generally, examine the behavior of employment and wages before and after buyouts. No wage data, and only data on total employment, have been available to previous investigators (e.g., Kaplan 1988). We analyze the following variables:

E_N = number of nonproduction workers,

E_P = number of production workers,

C_N = total annual compensation (wage bill) of nonproduction workers,

C_P = total annual compensation of production workers,

W_N = average annual compensation of nonproduction workers ($= C_N/E_N$),

W_P = average annual compensation of production workers ($= C_P/E_P$),

H_P = average annual man-hours of production workers,

W_P' = average hourly compensation of production workers ($= W_P/H_P$),

and the ratios E_N/E_P, C_N/C_P, and W_N/W_P.

We adopt the following procedure to perform the analysis. First, we standardize the natural logarithms of each variable by four-digit SIC industry and year. We then estimate equations of the following form:

$$Y_{i,t+k} - Y_{i,t+k-1} = (\Theta_k - \Theta_{k-1})BO_{i,t} + w_{i,t+k}, \qquad (2)$$

where Y is one of the standardized variables, and $k = -2, \ldots, 2$.[6] The expression $(\Theta_k - \Theta_{k-1})$ may be interpreted as the difference in growth rates from $t + k - 1$ to $t + k$ between plants involved in LBOs in year t and those not involved. To estimate the pre- versus postbuyout change, we calculate the sum $(\Theta_2 - \Theta_{-1}) = (\Theta_2 - \Theta_1) + (\Theta_1 - \Theta_0) + (\Theta_0 - \Theta_{-1})$; the expression $(\Theta_{-1} - \Theta_{-3}) = (\Theta_{-1} - \Theta_{-2}) + (\Theta_{-2} - \Theta_{-3})$ provides a prebuyout benchmark for comparison, and both are shown at the bottom of the table.

The estimates provide strong support for both implications of the hypothesis that LBOs are associated with the substitution of compensation for direct monitoring of production workers. First, between $t - 1$ and $t + 2$ there are sharp and significant reductions in nonproduction worker employment; the cumulative decline is 8.5 percent. Production-worker employment also appears to decline, but the declines are much smaller and not statistically significant. The estimates imply that the ratio of nonproduction to production employment declines 6.5 percent, relative to the industry average, in buyout plants.[7] Second, there are statistically significant increases in average production worker compensation (particularly annual compensation) between $t - 1$ and $t + 2$. The cumulative relative increases in annual and hourly compensation per production worker are 3.6 and 2.3 percent, respectively. In contrast, the annual compensation per nonproduction employee declines after the buyout. The ratio W_N/W_P declines 8.8 percent from $t - 1$ to $t + 2$, whereas it increases 3.3 percent from $t - 3$ to $t - 1$. As a result of this decline in relative compensation per worker, the ratio of nonproduction to production wage bills C_N/C_P declines even more than E_N/E_P, by 15.3 percent. The C_N/C_P ratio may be a better measure of the intensity of monitoring than E_N/E_P.

The decline in nonproduction employment could be offset by increases in employment in auxiliary establishments, so we have overstated the decline in the ratio of indirect or supervisory labor to production labor. But since only about one-fifth of white-collar manufacturing workers are employed in auxiliaries, the percentage increase in auxiliary employment required to offset the decline in nonproduction employment completely would have to be large. Moreover all of the anecdotal and econometric evidence suggests that control changes tend to reduce, rather than increase, auxiliary employment. It therefore seems more likely that our lack of data on auxiliaries results in an underestimate of the decline in the white-collar to blue-collar labor ratio, our indicator of the monitoring of production workers. But a definitive resolution of this issue must await the issuance of data on auxiliary establishments of firms before and after buyouts.

Table 5.6
Differences between LBO and non-LBO plants in mean growth rates (in percent) of labor variables, by period relative to year of LBO

Period	Growth rate during period											Number of LBO plants
	C_N	C_P	C_N/C_P	E_N	E_P	E_N/E_P	W_N	W_P	W_N/W_P	W'_P	H_P	
$t-3$ to $t-2$	3.5	−0.6	4.1	1.3	−0.0	1.3	2.2	−0.6	2.8	−0.0	−1.6	983
	(2.5)	(0.7)	(3.0)	(1.2)	(0.0)	(1.2)	(2.1)	(1.2)	(2.3)	(0.0)	(1.4)	
$t-2$ to $t-1$	−2.6	−0.3	−2.3	−2.7	0.1	−2.8	0.1	−0.4	0.5	0.6	−2.7	983
	(2.3)	(0.3)	(2.4)	(2.4)	(0.1)	(2.7)	(0.8)	(0.5)	(0.4)	(0.8)	(2.2)	
$t-1$ to t	−3.1	−0.4	−2.7	−3.1	−0.3	−2.8	−0.0	−0.1	0.1	0.0	−0.8	983
	(3.1)	(0.3)	(2.1)	(2.7)	(0.4)	(2.2)	(0.0)	(0.2)	(0.1)	(0.1)	(0.7)	
t to $t+1$	−3.4	0.8	−4.2	−3.3	−1.4	−1.9	−0.1	2.2	−2.3	1.7	−1.7	636
	(2.3)	(0.5)	(2.7)	(2.4)	(1.3)	(1.3)	(0.1)	(2.7)	(1.5)	(1.9)	(1.1)	
$t+1$ to $t+2$	−7.2	1.2	−8.4	−2.1	−0.3	−1.8	−5.1	1.5	−6.6	0.6	1.2	481
	(4.4)	(0.8)	(4.8)	(1.3)	(0.3)	(1.2)	(3.6)	(1.8)	(3.8)	(0.6)	(0.7)	
$t-3$ to $t-1$	0.9	−0.9	1.8	−1.4	0.1	−1.5	2.3	−1.0	3.3	0.6	−4.3	983
$t-1$ to $t+2$	−13.7	1.6	−15.3	−8.5	−2.0	−6.5	−5.2	3.6	−8.8	2.3	−1.3	481

Note: The sample is an extract of the Census Bureau's Longitudinal Research Database linked to Morgan Stanley data on LBOs and includes annual data for 1972–86 on 12,895 continuously observed manufacturing plants. Absolute values of t-statistics are in parentheses. The figures are estimates of the expression $(\Theta_k - \Theta_{k-1})$ from the equation

$$Y_{i,t+k} - Y_{i,t+k-1} = (\Theta_k - \Theta_{k-1})\mathrm{LBO}_{i,t} + w_{i,t+k},$$

where $Y_{i,t+k}$ is the value for plant i in year $t+k$ of the logarithm of one of the following variables, or of their ratios: E_N, number of nonproduction workers; E_P, number of production workers; C_N, total annual compensation (wage bill) of nonproduction workers; C_P, total annual compensation of production workers; W_N, annual compensation per nonproduction worker ($=C_N/E_N$); W_P, annual compensation per production worker ($=C_P/E_P$); H_P, average annual man-hours of production workers; or W'_P, compensation per production-worker man-hour ($=W_P/H_P$). $\mathrm{LBO}_{i,t}$ is equal to 1 if plant i was involved in any leveraged buyout in year t and otherwise equal to zero, and w is a disturbance. Before estimating the above equation, we standardized the Y values by four-digit SIC industry and year. The values of $\Theta_k - \Theta_{k-1}$ are multiplied by 100 and therefore represent differences between mean percentage changes (growth rates) of buyout and nonbuyout plants.

R&D Investment

About half of the R&D scientists and engineers employed in industry are located in auxiliary establishments rather than in production establishments. The most comprehensive and reliable information about industrial R&D comes from the National Science Foundation/Census Bureau's annual survey of industrial R&D: the RD-1 survey. This is a survey of firms rather than plants, and it forms the basis for the government's official statistics on industrial R&D investment and employment. In the RD-1 survey we have access to longitudinal data on R&D expenditure, sales, R&D employment, as well as total employment for over 1,200 firms.

Despite the relatively high quality of the RD-1 data, several difficulties are associated with using firm-level data to assess the impact of LBOs on R&D activity. First, such data cannot be used to gauge the effect of partial-firm LBOs, which account for 51 of the 131 LBOs in our sample. We estimate equations of the form

$$Y_{i,t+k} = \Theta_k BO_{i,t} + W_{i,t+k},\tag{3}$$

where Y is defined as R&D expenditure, to estimate the effect of LBOs on R&D, but we define $BO_{i,t}$ as follows: $BO_{i,t} = 1$ if firm i was involved in a complete-firm buyout in year t, and otherwise equals zero. Second, following a leveraged buyout, firms frequently sell off divisions, partly to pay down the debt incurred. Asset sales will artificially reduce the pre- versus postbuyout change in R&D expenditure and employment if the divisions that are sold were performing any R&D before the sale. We can attempt to reduce this downward bias by examining changes in R&D intensity—the ratio of R&D expenditure to sales, or of R&D employment to total employment—rather than in the level of R&D expenditure or employment, since the denominators as well as the numerators of these ratios are reduced by asset sales. It seems likely, however, that the divisions divested after the buyout are those that are more R&D intensive. Previous studies have documented, and our findings confirm, that targets of LBOs tend not to be R&D intensive because R&D-intensive businesses are not good buyout candidates. When a diversified firm is acquired in an LBO, the most R&D-intensive divisions therefore have a higher probability of being sold. If so, the pre- versus postbuyout change in R&D intensity will be biased downward.

Table 5.7 presents differences between the mean values of both R&D-intensity measures in year $t + k$ ($k = -7, \ldots, 5$) of companies involved in complete-firm LBOs in year t and those not involved. (The R&D-intensity

Table 5.7
Differences in mean R&D intensity (in percent) in year $t + k$ ($k = -7, \ldots, 5$) between firms involved in LBOs in year t and those not involved

Year	R&D expenditures/sales	R&D employment/ total employment
$t - 7$	−2.0	−1.0
	(0.97)	(1.32)
	[56/870]	[55/740]
$t - 6$	−2.2	−1.3
	(1.31)	(1.90)
	[60/850]	[59/722]
$t - 5$	−2.4	−1.7
	(1.23)	(2.41)
	[61/817]	[61/693]
$t - 4$	−2.5	−1.6
	(1.32)	(2.05)
	[63/1,283]	[62/956]
$t - 3$	−2.6	−1.9
	(1.53)	(2.16)
	[68/1,284]	[67/968]
$t - 2$	−2.7	−2.4
	(1.82)	(2.63)
	[68/1,214]	[67/922]
$t - 1$	−2.1	−2.2
	(1.27)	(2.22)
	[68/1,224]	[67/955]
t	−2.6	−2.3
	(1.30)	(1.82)
	[68/1,261]	[67/1,005]
$t + 1$	−3.0	−2.8
	(1.39)	(1.75)
	[56/1,272]	[55/1,024]
$t + 2$	−2.9	−2.6
	(1.24)	(1.43)
	[39/1,282]	[38/1,110]
$t + 3$	−3.9	−3.2
	(0.74)	(1.35)
	[24/2,227]	[23/1,908]
$t + 4$	−1.9	−3.0
	(0.45)	(1.09)
	[8/2,254]	[7/2,072]
$t + 5$	−3.1	−3.4
	(0.34)	(0.84)
	[4/2,336]	[3/2,161]

Source: Longitudinal data on R&D expenditure, sales, R&D employment, and total employment from the National Science Foundation/Census Bureau annual surveys of industrial R&D for 1972–86, linked to a Morgan Stanley and Co. list of all LBOs during 1979–88 whose value exceeds $35 million.
Note: Absolute values of t-statistics are in parentheses. Number of LBO firms/total number of firms are in brackets.

measures in the table are not standardized by industry; standardized data are examined in table 5.8.) We wish to make several observations about the estimates in table 5.7. First, firms involved in LBOs are much less R&D intensive than other firms before the LBO.[8] The mean ratio of R&D expenditure to sales for non-LBO firms is about 3.5 percent during the 1981–86 period. From $t - 3$ to $t - 1$ the average difference between means of this ratio for the LBO firm and non-LBO firm is -2.5 percent, implying a mean LBO firm ratio of 1.0 percent. Second, the LBO versus non-LBO difference is larger in the three years after than in the three years before the buyout. The average difference for $t + 1$ to $t + 3$ is -3.2 percent, a decline of 0.7 percent; the R&D employment intensity measure also declines by 0.7 percent. The pre- versus postbuyout changes in these differences are not statistically significant, however. Third, the relative R&D intensity of LBO firms appears to have been declining in the years before the buyout. This is particularly evident with the R&D-employment-intensity measure: The mean LBO versus non-LBO difference declines from -1.0 percent in $t - 7$ to -2.4 percent in $t - 1$. But this change is also not significant.

Table 5.8 provides another perspective on the effects of LBOs on R&D activity, in the form of estimates of Θ_{-1}, and Θ'_k from the following equations:

$$\ln Z_{i,t-1} = \Theta_{-1} BO_{i,t} + W_{i,t-1}, \tag{4}$$

$$\ln Z_{i,t+k} = \Theta'_k BO_{i,t} + \pi_k \ln Z_{i,t-1} + W'_{i,t+k}, \tag{5}$$

where Z is defined as either R&D expenditure, sales, or R&D intensity (the ratio of R&D expenditure to sales), and $BO_{i,t}$ equals 1 if firm i was involved in a full-firm buyout in year t, and otherwise equals zero.[9] The logarithms of these variables were standardized by primary industry of the firm and year before estimating these equations. Some firms have zero R&D expenditure in some years; these observations are excluded from the R&D-expenditure and R&D-intensity regressions but not from the sales regressions (nor were they excluded in table 5.7), so the coefficients in a given row need not add up.

The estimates of Θ_{-1} reveal that the mean R&D expenditure of LBO firms in year $t - 1$ is 45 percent higher than that of non-LBO firms in the same industry, but their mean sales are 97 percent higher, so their mean R&D intensity is 49 percent lower. LBO targets tend to be less R&D intensive before the LBO than other firms in their industries, as well as disproportionately in non-R&D-intensive industries. In fact the within-industry difference accounts for about two-thirds of the total (within- plus

Table 5.8
Differences in levels and growth rates of R&D intensity, R&D expenditure, and sales, between buyout and non-buyout firms

Parameter	R&D expenditures/ sales	R&D expenditures	Sales	Number of firms LBO/total
Θ_{-1}	−48.6 (2.24)	44.8 (1.23)	97.4 (3.42)	68/1,363
Θ'_1	−1.8 (0.13)	−5.6 (0.44)	−7.9 (0.63)	56/1,241
Θ'_2	−17.1 (0.83)	−25.6 (1.28)	−10.9 (0.68)	36/1,241
Θ'_3	−25.9 (0.75)	−5.1 (0.15)	−15.1 (0.52)	24/1,243
Θ'_4	0.7 (0.02)	11.3 (0.26)	−1.4 (0.04)	8/1,246
Θ'_5	−46.7 (0.42)	32.3 (1.40)	61.3 (0.57)	4/1,299

Note: t-statistics are in parentheses. The figures are estimates of the parameters Θ_{-1} and Θ'_k from the following equations:

$$\ln Z_{i,t-1} = \Theta_{-1} \, \text{LBO}_{i,t} + w_{i,t-1},$$

$$\ln Z_{i,t+k} = \Theta'_k \, \text{LBO}_{i,t} + \pi_k \ln Z_{i,t-1} + w'_{i,t+k},$$

where $Z_{i,t+k}$ is the value for firm i in year $t + k$ of R&D expenditure, sales, or intensity (the ratio of R&D expenditure to sales), and $\text{LBO}_{i,t}$ equals 1 if firm i was involved in a full-firm leveraged buyout in year t and otherwise equals zero. We standardized the logarithms of each of these variables by primary industry of the firm and year before estimating these equations. The parameter estimates are multiplied by 100 and are based on longitudinal data from the National Science Foundation/Census Bureau annual surveys of industrial R&D for 1972–86, linked to a Morgan Stanley and Co. list of all LBOs during 1979–88 whose value exceeds $35 million.

between-industry) difference between LBO and non-LBO R&D intensity revealed in table 5.7.

The estimates of Θ'_k corresponding to all three variables are negative for $k = 1$ to 3, but none are statistically significant. (The standard errors of the estimates corresponding to years $t + 4$ and $t + 5$ are again particularly large, so we won't discuss these estimates.) Thus these estimates, like those in table 5.7, imply that we cannot reject the hypothesis of no change in relative R&D intensity from one year before to one to three years after the buyout. Also, consistent with our discussion of postbuyout divestitures, the mean relative decline in R&D expenditure is greater than the decline in R&D intensity for $k = 1$ and 2, and less than the decline in sales for $k = 3$.

Summary and Conclusions

We investigate the effects of leveraged buyouts on productivity and related variables using a large, longitudinal, plant-level data base that includes plants belonging to both privately and publicly owned firms. We argue that total factor productivity is perhaps the purest measure of technical efficiency and cite economic theories that imply that TFP is an important determinant of key economic and financial variables such as profits, stock prices, per capita output, inflation, and real wages.

The buyouts in our sample all occurred during the years 1981–86. We initially pool the data across all years, thus constraining the productivity effects of buyouts occurring in different calendar years to be identical. For example, we constrain the effect of a buyout of a plant in 1981 on its 1983 productivity to be equal to the effect of a buyout of a plant in 1984 on its 1986 productivity. The constrained estimates indicate that productivity is significantly higher in the first three years after the buyout than in any of the eight years before the buyout, even though buyout plants are already more efficient than nonbuyout plants before the transaction. The difference in mean productivity between plants involved in LBOs in year t and those not involved is 1.7 percent for years $t - 3$ to $t - 1$ and 3.9 percent for years $t + 1$ to $t + 3$. The corresponding difference in median productivity is 2.3 percent for years $t - 3$ to $t - 1$ and 5.9 percent for years $t + 1$ to $t + 3$.

The pre- versus postbuyout increase in mean productivity is greater for plants involved in management buyouts (from 4.3 to 10.2 percent), but the increase in median productivity of MBO plants (from 3.2 to 6.4 percent) is about the same as the median increase for all LBO plants. (The estimates also reveal that the efficiency of plants involved in MBOs in year t increases sharply before the buyout, from $t - 4$ to $t - 1$.)

The differences between the mean or median productivity of buyout and nonbuyout plants in years $t + 4$ and $t + 5$ are not significant, however, and in some cases are negative. The finding that the coefficients for the years $t + 1$ to $t + 3$ are significantly greater than the coefficients for $t - 3$ to $t - 1$, whereas the coefficients for $t + 4$ and $t + 5$ are not, could reflect a transitory positive impact on TFP that vanishes, and perhaps even becomes negative, after three years. But further analysis reveals that this feature of the estimates is primarily an artifact of pooling the data across calendar years. The contrast between the $t + 1$ to $t + 3$ estimates and the $t + 4$ to $t + 5$ estimates is due to differences between the productivity effect of early (1981–82) and later (1983–86) buyouts rather than to the tendency of productivity to decline after a typical buyout.

Apparently the 38 LBOs that occurred in 1981 and 1982 did not have a significant effect on productivity in any postbuyout year. In sharp contrast, post-1982 LBOs had an impact in years $t + 1$ to $t + 3$ even greater than that implied by the pooled estimates. The late LBO coefficients also show an upward trend after the buyout: The $t + 3$ coefficient is about twice as large as the $t + 1$ and $t + 2$ coefficients.

For management buyouts the contrast between early and late buyout effects is somewhat different, although these estimates are much less precise. The early MBOs apparently had a strong positive impact on productivity in $t + 1$—indeed stronger than the $t + 1$ impact of later MBOs. But the early MBO impact was insignificant and/or negative (and tended to decline) in years $t + 2$ to $t + 5$, whereas the impact of late MBOs was positive, significant, and increasing from $t + 1$ to $t + 3$. Explanation of the difference between the productivity impact of early and later buyouts is a task for future research.

The analysis reveals that productivity is significantly higher in the first three years after a post-1982 buyout than it was before the buyout, but we cannot prove that the buyout was the cause of the productivity gain. The fact that the productivity increase is accompanied by other changes, however, such as a reduction in the ratio of white-collar to blue-collar labor that is likely to be caused by the LBO, casts doubt on the proposition that the productivity increase would have occurred in the absence of, or in fact caused, the LBO.

The estimates summarized above are based only on surviving plants. We investigated the possibility that the relative productivity of surviving buyout plants increases during the first three postbuyout years because of a lower survival rate among buyout plants but find no support for this hypothesis: The survival rate in years t to $t + 3$ is slightly (but not significantly) higher for plants involved in buyouts in year t than for those not involved.

We use data on employment and compensation of both production and nonproduction workers (including supervisory employees above the working-supervisor level) to investigate whether Jensen's hypothesis concerning the substitution by LBO associations of compensation for direct monitoring applies to production workers. The data are consistent with both implications of this hypothesis. The ratio of nonproduction to production worker employment (wage bill) of buyout plants declines 6.5 percent (15.3 percent) from $t - 1$ to $t + 2$. Also there are significant increases in both the hourly and especially the annual rates of compensation of production workers in buyout plants during this interval, of 2.3 percent and 3.6 percent, respectively. The decline in nonproduction employment could be offset by increases in employment in auxiliary establishments (which are excluded from our sample). In that sense we might have overstated the decline in the ratio of supervisory labor to production labor. But all of the anecdotal and econometric evidence suggests that control changes tend to reduce auxiliary employment, so in fact we might have underestimated the decline in the white-collar to blue-collar labor ratio, our indicator of the monitoring of production workers.

Finally, we examine the impact of full-firm LBOs on R&D activity using longitudinal firm-level data collected in the government's annual survey of industrial R&D. We confirm the finding of previous studies that LBO targets are much less R&D intensive than other firms. There are two reasons for this: LBO targets tend to be in non-R&D-intensive industries, and their R&D intensity tends to be below the industry average. The mean relative R&D intensity of buyout firms is lower in the three years after than in the three years before the buyout. The change in R&D intensity is far from statistically significant, however. This change will be biased downward if the most R&D-intensive units of the firm tend to be sold off, which is plausible. Also the relative R&D intensity of buyout firms appears to have been declining for a number of years before the buyout.

6   U.S. and Foreign Mergers and LBOs, 1988–90

In chapter 3 we analyzed the total-factor productivity of U.S. manufacturing establishments involved in ownership changes (mergers and acquisitions) during the period 1972–81, using Census Bureau data. One important finding was that plants changing owners in year t were significantly less efficient in year $t - 1$ than other plants in the same industry. We argued that this might be attributable to poor management of the plant by the incumbent owner because of a bad match between the two. There was also some evidence that the relative efficiency of target plants had declined in the years preceding the ownership change: Mean productivity fell from -2.6 percent in year $t - 7$ to -3.7 percent in year $t - 1$.

In chapter 5 we performed a similar analysis for plants involved in leveraged buyouts during the period 1981–86. We found that their relative performance before the buyout was very different from the premerger performance of plants involved in mergers and acquisitions. The productivity of plants involved in LBOs was significantly above average in the three years preceding the buyout. Moreover there were no signs of a decline in this efficiency advantage prior to the buyout; indeed the mean productivity of MBO plants increased sharply just before the buyout.

In this chapter we reexamine the performance of enterprises involved in mergers, acquisitions, and leveraged buyouts, using a new data set, the Global Vantage Industrial/Commercial (GVIC) file, which differs from our earlier ones in a variety of important respects.

Country and sectoral coverage. The file includes data for as many as 5,448 relatively large publicly traded industrial and commercial (not just manufacturing) companies from over 30 countries.

Time period. The GVIC contains fairly complete data for the years 1982–89, although all of the mergers, acquisitions, and LBOs reported in the file occurred after April 1987.

Unit of analysis (level of aggregation). The GVIC is a firm- rather than establishment-level file.

Type of data. The file contains over 200 income statement, balance sheet, flow of funds, and supplemental data items.

Because the GVIC file has these properties, we can use it to assess whether our findings based on older data for the United States only also apply to more recent transactions both in the United States and overseas. Due to the nature of the available data, however, the analysis in this chapter will differ from that in previous chapters in two major respects. First, rather than TFP, the measure of performance that we will use is profitability, or the after-tax rate of return on fixed assets, defined as the ratio of net income to gross tangible fixed assets.[1] As noted in chapter 1, some theoretical models imply that profitability is determined by, and an increasing function of, productivity, so firms' relative profitability may be a reasonable (albeit noisy) indicator of their relative productivity.

The second difference vis-à-vis previous chapters is that the GVIC file enables us to observe firms before, but not after, the merger, acquisition, or leveraged buyout. Previous chapters provided support for the following hypotheses: (1) The relative performance of firms improves following a merger or acquisition and eventually "catches up" to the industry average; (2) the relative performance of firms increases (even more) following a leveraged buyout to a level significantly above the industry average. These hypotheses cannot be tested with the GVIC file, since no financial data are reported for companies after they have merged or been acquired or bought out.[2]

Although the GVIC data do not permit us to measure the post-transaction segment of the performance trajectory for recent domestic and foreign corporate control transactions, and therefore to validate all of the hypotheses supported by our earlier data, they do enable estimation of the pretransaction segment, hence validation of some of those hypotheses. Because the coverage, timing, nature of the data, and the performance measure are quite different from those used in previous chapters, we believe pursuit of even this limited objective to be worthwhile.

International Comparisons of the Rate of Merger Activity

Table 6.1 presents data derived from the GVIC file on merger and acquisition activity by country.[3] The file contains annual data for the years 1982–90. The number of firms for which data were reported in at least one

Table 6.1
Merger rates by country: Firms merged or acquired in January 1988–November 1990

Country	Percent of firms merged and acquired	Number of mergers and acquisitions	Number of firms
New Zealand	18.7	6	32
Sweden	15.1	13	86
Australia	14.1	21	149
United Kingdom	12.9	90	696
Finland	8.1	3	37
Canada	7.9	24	305
United States	7.8	214	2,754
Belgium	7.0	4	57
Denmark	6.7	5	75
Norway	6.7	4	60
Hong Kong	5.3	3	57
Ireland	3.7	2	54
Spain	3.5	2	56
France	3.3	6	180
Switzerland	1.8	2	111
Italy	1.8	2	114
South Africa	0.8	1	126
Germany	0.5	1	189
Japan	0.3	2	633
Malaysia	0.0	0	54
Netherlands	0.0	0	60
Singapore	0.0	0	58
All countries	6.8	406	5,987

Note: Data reported are only for those countries with 30 or more firms represented in the Global Vantage Industrial/Commercial File.

year was 5,987. The year in which the largest number of companies (5,448) had data reported was 1987. Almost half (2,754) of the companies are American; the countries with the next largest representations are the United Kingdom (696), Japan (633), and Canada (305).

Four hundred and six (6.8 percent) of these companies merged or were acquired at some time during the period January 1988 to November 1990. Slightly more than half (53 percent) of these transactions involved U.S. firms. Almost half (47 percent) of the foreign transactions involved British firms, and Canada, Australia, and Sweden accounted for most of the rest.

The countries with the highest rates of merger and acquisition activity are the current and former members of the British Commonwealth (New Zealand, Australia, the United Kingdom, and Canada) and the Scandinavian countries (Sweden and to a lesser extent Finland, Norway, and Denmark). The United States ranked 7 out of 22 countries with respect to merger rate. The merger rate of the United States was 15 times that of Germany and 24 times that of Japan.

The Relative Profitability of Firms prior to Merger or Acquisition

To investigate the relative profitability of firms prior to merger or acquisition, we adopted the following procedure. For each firm in each year we calculated the ratio of net income after taxes to gross tangible fixed assets. To avoid the possibility that our results would be driven by a few extreme observations (outliers), we trimmed the sample by eliminating observations for which the absolute value of this ratio exceeded unity. Next we standardized the profitability data by country and year by subtracting from each observation the mean profitability value of all firms in the same country and year. The transformed data are therefore deviations from country and year means.[4] We then eliminated from the sample firms that did not merge or were not acquired. For the remaining firms we determined the year in which the merger or acquisition occurred, and for each observation calculated the relative year, namely, the data year minus the year of the transaction. For example, if firm X merged in 1988, then the value of relative year for firm X in 1984 was -4. Finally, we computed the mean (and median) value of normalized profitability for each value of relative year.

Estimates of normalized productivity in years $t-8$ to $t-1$ are presented in table 6.2. The left-hand panel displays estimates based on pooled data for all countries. The sample is "unbalanced" in the sense that the number of firms is different in different relative years: It increases from

Table 6.2
Normalized profitability in years $t - 8$ to t of firms merged or acquired in year t

Year	All countries			United States only			Foreign only		
	Mean	Median	N	Mean	Median	N	Mean	Median	N
$t - 8$	-0.007 (0.32)	-0.017	78	0.023 (0.69)	-0.032	33	-0.030 (0.94)	-0.006	45
$t - 7$	-0.003 (0.20)	-0.020	230	0.011 (0.47)	-0.044	95	-0.013 (0.77)	-0.017	135
$t - 6$	-0.003 (0.22)	-0.027	301	-0.008 (0.40)	-0.036	147	0.003 (0.20)	-0.017	154
$t - 5$	0.013 (1.06)	-0.023	318	0.016 (0.79)	-0.020	158	0.009 (0.73)	-0.023	160
$t - 4$	0.001 (0.06)	-0.022	341	0.010 (0.47)	-0.017	174	-0.008 (0.64)	-0.033	167
$t - 3$	-0.004 (0.32)	-0.032	364	-0.003 (0.16)	-0.022	188	-0.005 (0.35)	-0.036	176
$t - 2$	-0.022 (1.70)	-0.029	364	-0.024 (1.16)	-0.028	190	-0.021 (1.29)	-0.039	174
$t - 1$	-0.031 (1.83)	-0.018	235	-0.057 (2.41)	-0.023	156	0.020 (1.09)	-0.003	79
t	-0.073 (0.59)	-0.061	9	-0.079 (0.56)	-0.071	8			

Note: t-statistics to test H_0: mean = 0 are in parentheses. Normalized profitability is the firm's ratio of net income to assets minus the mean value of that ratio for all firms in the same country and calendar year.

$t - 8$ to $t - 2$ and then declines. (Estimates based on a "balanced" sample will be presented below.) The sample means for the years $t - 8$ to $t - 3$ are all insignificantly different from zero, indicating that we cannot reject the hypothesis that the performance of these firms was average during these years. However, the means decline monotonically from $t - 5$ to t and are significantly negative in years $t - 2$ and $t - 1$. These estimates suggest that the profitability of firms begins to decline about five years before they merge or are acquired and that this decline accelerates two or three years before the transaction. The medians are also negative in the years preceding the control change, but they are negative in all eight years and unlike the means, do not exhibit a negative trend.

The middle and right-hand panels of table 6.2 present separate estimates for U.S. and foreign transactions. The estimates for the United States are qualitatively similar to the full-sample estimates. The main difference is that the United States mean for year $t - 1$ is much larger in magnitude and more significant than the corresponding mean for all countries. The U.S. estimates imply that not only does relative profitability decline from $t - 5$ to $t - 1$, it declines at an accelerating rate: The first-difference in these means for the years $t - 4$ to $t - 1$ are -0.006, -0.013, -0.021, and -0.033.

The foreign estimates are more equivocal. None of the means are significant at conventional significance levels. The medians are negative and nonincreasing for the years $t - 8$ to $t - 2$, again suggesting poor and deteriorating performance, but both mean and median increase from $t - 2$ to $t - 1$. The $t - 1$ sample, however, is less than half the size of the $t - 2$ sample, so this comparison may be quite distorted.

Table 6.3 presents estimates of mean and median levels and changes in normalized productivity based on a balanced panel of firms. The top panel displays estimates of the levels in the years $t - 5$ and $t - 1$ and the change between those years. (The sample mean change provides a more powerful test of the null hypothesis of "no change in profitablity from $t - 5$ to $t - 1$" than the change in sample means.) The estimate for all countries leads to a decisive rejection of that hypothesis: Normalized profitability declines by 5.7 percentage points, and the t-statistic is 2.44. The estimates are consistent with the following characterization: Five years before the merger or acquisition, profitability is about average—indeed slightly (not significantly) above average. Then the firm's performance is subjected to a serious negative shock. As a result just prior to the transaction the firm's performance is well below the average of other firms in the country.

Table 6.3
Change in normalized profitability from year $t-5$ to $t-1$ or $t-2$, of firms merged or acquired in year t

Year or period	All countries			United States only			Foreign only		
	Mean	Median	N	Mean	Median	N	Mean	Median	N
$t-5$	0.014 (0.83)	−0.020	182	0.015 (0.62)	−0.012	117	0.013 (0.62)	−0.034	65
$(t-1)-$ $(t-5)$	−0.057 (2.44)	−0.018	182	−0.098 (2.84)	−0.046	117	0.016 (0.80)	0.015	65
$t-1$	−0.043 (2.31)	−0.023	182	−0.083 (3.17)	−0.040	117	0.029 (1.47)	0.003	65
$t-5$	0.010 (0.81)	−0.025	289	0.009 (0.45)	−0.021	146	0.011 (0.79)	−0.026	143
$(t-2)-$ $(t-5)$	−0.040 (2.83)	−0.021	289	−0.054 (2.41)	−0.026	146	−0.026 (1.51)	−0.014	143
$t-2$	−0.030 (2.32)	−0.030	289	−0.044 (2.24)	−0.035	146	−0.015 (0.91)	−0.029	143

Note: t-statistics to test H_0: mean $= 0$ are in parentheses. Normalized profitability is the firm's ratio of net income to assets minus the mean value of that ratio for all firms in the same country and calendar year.

The middle panel of table 6.3 reveals that the decline in performance from $t - 5$ to $t - 1$, and the consequent profitability deficit in year $t - 1$, is much larger and more significant for U.S. firms: Their after-tax rate of return declines by almost ten percentage points, relative to the U.S. average, during those four years. For foreign firms both the change in profitability from $t - 5$ to $t - 1$ and the level of profitability in $t - 1$ are positive and insignificant. We have previously noted, however, that the size of the foreign sample drops substantially from $t - 2$ to $t - 1$, so these estimates should be regarded with caution. In the bottom panel of the table, we present an alternative set of estimates based on the period $t - 5$ to $t - 2$ instead of $t - 5$ to $t - 1$. In this case the foreign estimates of both the change and the final level are negative, but the foreign estimates are less negative than the U.S. estimates and are not significant.

Since the number of American companies is much greater than the number of sample firms from each of the other countries and since the data were standardized by country, the normalized profitability data might be more reliable for U.S. firms than for foreign firms. This could lead to larger standard errors on the foreign means than on the U.S. means. But it would account for little, if any, of the difference between the U.S. and foreign results. The point estimates for foreign firms of the change and final level of profitability are at best (based on $t - 2$) much smaller in magnitude than—and at worst (based on $t - 1$) opposite in sign from—the corresponding U.S. estimates. We therefore conclude that unlike U.S. mergers and acquisitions, foreign mergers and acquisitions do not tend to be preceded by a marked deterioration in the profitability of the target firm. In this sense these transactions appear to play different roles in U.S. and foreign capital markets.

The Relative Profitability of Firms Prior to Leveraged Buyout

In chapter 5 we presented evidence that leveraged buyouts were different in several respects from garden-variety mergers and acquisitions. In particular, we found that U.S. mergers and acquisitions are preceded by below-average performance (productivity), whereas leveraged buyouts are usually preceeded by above-average firm performance. We have just corroborated the first finding (for U.S., but not for foreign, companies); we now attempt briefly to corroborate the second.

Twenty of the companies (all of them American) in the GVIC file were acquired via leveraged buyout in 1987 or later. Table 6.4 presents normalized profitability estimates for these companies. Since the LBO sample size

Table 6.4
Normalized profitability in years $t - 6$ to $t - 1$ of firms involved in leveraged buyouts in year t

Year	Mean	Median	N
$t - 6$	0.044 (0.72)	0.008	16
$t - 5$	0.030 (0.48)	−0.042	14
$t - 4$	0.034 (0.57)	0.031	18
$t - 3$	0.086 (1.47)	0.043	19
$t - 2$	0.044 (1.13)	−0.010	20
$t - 1$	0.026 (0.47)	−0.010	17

Note: t-statistics to test H_0: mean = 0 are in parentheses. Normalized profitability is the firm's ratio of net income to assets minus the mean value of that ratio for all firms in the same country and calendar year.

is much smaller than the sample size for other mergers and acquisitions, the standard errors in this table are much larger than those in the previous two tables. Nevertheless, the means convey the strong impression that LBOs tend to be preceeded by above-average profitability: All of the means are positive, and the mean for year $t - 3$ is close to being significant. These results therefore appear to confirm our findings in the previous chapter about pre-LBO productivity at the plant level.

Summary and Conclusions

In this chapter we reexamined the performance of firms involved in mergers, acquisitions, and leveraged buyouts using a new and very different data base that includes information on both U.S. and foreign firms involved in corporate control changes since 1988. Although the sample period, coverage, level of aggregation, and measure of performance differ from those used in previous chapters, the empirical results for U.S. firms are quite consistent with our earlier results.

American firms that merge or are acquired tend to be formerly healthy firms whose financial condition has deteriorated, sometimes at an accelerating rate, prior to the transaction. From year $t - 5$ to $t - 1$ their after-tax rate of return on fixed assets declines almost ten percentage points, from slightly above average to significantly below average. Since another firm is willing to acquire these assets, presumably the lapse or decline in performance is perceived by the acquiror to be, to use Hirschman's term, "repairable." Mergers and acquisitions may therefore serve as "mechanisms of recuperation [that] play a most useful role in avoiding social losses as well as human hardship."[5]

It is tempting to draw a biological analogy: Organisms that have become weak are ingested by, and nourish, healthy organisms. This process presumably contributes to the survival and success of the ecosystem (economic system) as a whole.

Foreign mergers and acquisitions, and U.S. leveraged buyouts, tend not to be preceded by the declines in performance associated with U.S. mergers and acquisitions. The profitability of foreign merger and acquisition targets is not significantly below average immediately before the transaction. If the profitability of these firms has declined at all, it has declined much less than that of U.S. targets. It is not clear to us why the U.S. and foreign premerger performance trajectories differ in this important respect.

Firm-level profitability data on post-1987 leveraged buyouts were consistent with plant-level productivity data on pre-1987 LBOs: The firms that are bought out tend to be above-average performers prior to the transaction. Below-average performers are unlikely LBO targets.

The Dismantling of Conglomerate Firms

This chapter examines another means by which changes in corporate control may bring about improvements in operating efficiency: by reducing the extent of industrial diversification, namely, the number of industries in which a firm operates. During the quarter century following the Second World War, U.S. industrial enterprises became increasingly diversified. Rumelt[1] has estimated that the percentage of diversified companies in the Fortune 500 more than doubled from 1949 to 1974, from under 30 percent to over 60 percent. The greatest increase in the extent of diversification apparently occurred during the conglomerate merger wave of the late 1960s, which Golbe and White (1988) have shown to be the most intense period of merger and acquisition (M&A) activity between 1940 and 1985.

The extent of industrial diversification probably peaked in the early 1970s. As Ravenscraft and Scherer (1987) have documented, by the mid-1970s conglomerate firms began to divest the unrelated (to their primary industry) lines of business they had acquired during the 1960s. A substantial fraction of the corporate control transactions of the 1970s were divestitures of previously acquired units.

Our previous research suggested the existence of the following causal relationship:

$$\text{Control changes} \xrightarrow{(+)} \text{productivity,} \tag{1}$$

where the $(+)$ above the arrow denotes a positive relationship. We will attempt to establish that the sign of this "reduced form" relationship is positive in part because of the (negative) signs of the "structural" relationships between these two variables and a mediating variable:

$$\text{Control changes} \xrightarrow{(-)} \text{diversification} \xrightarrow{(-)} \text{productivity.} \tag{2}$$

In other words, control changes of the 1970s and 1980s led to increases in productivity in part because these changes (unlike the control changes of the earlier postwar era, particularly the late 1960s) reduced the extent of industrial diversification, and diversification is inversely related to productivity.

Our first objective will be to provide empirical support for the second of the two hypotheses indicated in (2) above, the one concerning the effect of diversification on productivity. Several previous studies have examined the effect of diversification on other measures of firm performance, such as profitability, Tobin's q, and shareholder wealth. Ravenscraft and Scherer (1987) found that unrelated lines of business acquired during the conglomerate merger boom of the late 1960s experienced below-average profitability in the 1970s and were often subsequently divested. Wernerfelt and Montgomery (1988) found that "narrowly diversified firms do better [have higher values of q, ceteris paribus] than widely diversified firms." Morck, Shleifer, and Vishny (1989a) found that diversification reduced bidding firms' shareholder wealth in the 1980s, although it failed to do so in the 1970s. However, we are not aware of any previous research on the effect of diversification on TFP (output per unit of total input) which is generally regarded by economists as the purest measure of technical efficiency. We will estimate this effect using rich and detailed Census Bureau data from 1980 for over 17,000 manufacturing establishments.

Our investigation of the first hypothesis indicated in (2), concerning the effects of (recent) control changes on the extent of diversification, will be based on a different data set and will be less direct. Using Compustat data, we will describe and analyze changes between January 1985 and November 1989 in the distribution of companies by the number of industries in which they operate. Due to data limitations control changes will not be explicitly accounted for in this analysis. But since the 1980s was a period of high and accelerating takeover activity—the value of takeover transactions as a fraction of GNP increased from 1.5 percent in 1979 to 4.5 percent in 1986—takeovers are probably responsible for much of the change in the extent of diversification.

Industrial Diversification and Productivity of Manufacturing Plants

To examine the effect of diversification on productivity, we use Census Bureau data on over 17,000 manufacturing establishments for 1980. As a measure of productivity differences among establishments, we use residuals from a production function estimated separately by four-digit SIC industry:

$$\ln VQ_{Oj} = \beta_{0j} + \beta_{Lj} \ln L_{ij}$$

$$+ \beta_{Kj} \ln K_{ij} + \beta_{Mj} \ln VM_{ij} + u_{ij} \qquad (3)$$

where VQ denotes the value of production (the value of shipments adjusted for changes in finished-goods and work-in-process inventories), L denotes labor input (production-worker-equivalent man-hours), K denotes capital input (the perpetual inventory estimate of the net stock of plant and equipment), VM denotes the value of materials consumed (materials purchased adjusted for changes in raw materials inventories), u is a disturbance term, and the subscript ij refers to establishment i in four-digit industry j. As discussed in chapter 2, the residual for a given observation measures the percentage deviation of that establishment's TFP from the mean TFP of all establishments in the same industry.

The basic premise is that the extent of parent-firm diversification influences the productivity of its plants.[2] To get at this relationship, we will compute weighted[3] regressions of variants of the following model:

$$\text{RESIDUAL} = \alpha_0 + \alpha_1 \ln(\text{NINDS}) + \alpha_2 \text{ SAMEIND}$$

$$+ \alpha_3 \ln(\text{NPLANTS}) + \alpha_4 \text{ SINGLE}$$

$$+ \alpha_5 \text{ AUXSHARE} + \alpha_6 \ln(\text{PLANTEMP}) + v, \qquad (4)$$

where RESIDUAL is the estimated residual from equation (3); NINDS is the total number of four-digit SIC manufacturing industries in which the firm operates; SAMEIND is the fraction of the firm's plants that operate in the same industry as this plant; NPLANTS is the total number of manufacturing plants owned and operated by the firm; SINGLE is a dummy variable equal to one if the firm operates only one plant, and otherwise equal to zero; AUXSHARE is the fraction of the parent firm's workers employed in auxiliary establishments, such as corporate headquarters and R&D labs; PLANTEMP is the number of workers employed in the plant; and v is a disturbance.

We are primarily concerned with the effects of the first two regressors: $\ln(\text{NINDS})$, an index of the degree of diversification, and SAMEIND, an index of specialization (the inverse of diversification) in the plant's industry. The remaining variables are included as "controls" because they are attributes of the firm or plant that may be correlated with the first two regressors and that may influence plant productivity (or proxy for variables that influence it).

Demsetz (1973) and Peltzman (1977) have provided evidence that the largest firms in a given industry—presumably, the firms operating the greatest number of plants in the industry—tend to be more efficient than smaller firms in the same industry. The explanation they propose for this is that firms that enjoy cost advantages (resulting from their having above-average values of unobservable variables such as managerial competence, success at innovating, or even luck) will tend to expand (e.g., by operating more plants). Their findings can be represented by a function of the form RESIDUAL $= f(NSAME)$, where $f' > 0$ and NSAME denotes the number of plants operated by the parent in the same industry as this plant. Demsetz and Peltzman did not explicitly consider the issue of diversification; we wish to do so by generalizing the preceding function to also include NOTHER ($= NPLANTS - NSAME$), the number of plants operated by the parent in other industries: RESIDUAL $= f(NSAME, NOTHER)$. We expect that the effect of NOTHER on RESIDUAL will be smaller than the effect of NSAME on RESIDUAL—it may even be zero—and want to formally test this hypothesis. A convenient way to do so is to specify the productivity-determination equation to take the form RESIDUAL $= \beta \log[NOTHER + (1 + \pi)NSAME]$ + other regressors, where π is the percentage difference between the productivity effect of NOTHER and NSAME. The preceding equation is nonlinear, but it can be approximated by the linear equation RESIDUAL $\approx \beta$ NPLANTS $+ \beta\pi$ SAMEIND + other regressors, where SAMEIND $\equiv NSAME/NPLANTS$ is the fraction of plants in the same industry. The ratio of the SAMEIND coefficient to the NPLANTS coefficient may be interpreted as an estimate of π, and the significance of π may be inferred from the t-statistic on the SAMEIND coefficient.

Thus, by including NPLANTS and SAMEIND in the model, we are allowing both NSAME and NOTHER to influence productivity, and allowing their marginal effects to be different. Inclusion of these variables is also necessary to obtain a consistent estimate of the effect of NINDS on productivity, since NPLANTS, for example, is likely to be strongly positively correlated with NINDS: Firms owning more plants are likely to operate in more industries. If $\alpha_3 > 0$ and corr(NINDS, NPLANTS) > 0, failure to include NPLANTS in equation (4) would result in an upwardly biased estimate of α_1 and/or α_2. The same argument applies to the variable SINGLE, since it is an alternative (or additional) proxy for the size of the parent.

AUXSHARE is included because failure to account for auxiliary inputs could result in seriously distorted estimates of plant productivity (see chapter 4), and these distortions are likely to be strongly correlated with our measures of firm industrial structure. PLANTEMP is included to control for possible effects of scale on productivity, although the production function (3) already is not constrainted to constant returns to scale (since the input coefficients do not have to sum to one).

The ultimate source of the data is the 1980 Annual Survey of Manufactures (ASM). Due to the way in which our sample was drawn from the ASM, some of the regressors of equation (4) are measured with error. Although the measurement error is not of the classical (e.g., normal, i.i.d.) form, one suspects that it would bias the coefficients and t-statistics on these variables toward zero.

Descriptive statistics for our sample of 17,664 plants are provided in table 7.1. The correlation coefficients among the three variables NPLANTS, NINDS, and SAMEIND have the expected signs (large firms tend to be more diversified), and their magnitudes are large (above 0.8).

Weighted least-squares regressions of the plant productivity RESIDUAL on plant and parent firm characteristics are displayed in table 7.2. Each column of the table represents a separate regression. The regression in the first column includes one of our two indicators of the extent of diversification, $\ln(NINDS)$, as well as the four control variables $\ln(NPLANTS)$, SINGLE, AUXSHARE, and $\ln(PLANTEMP)$. The coefficient on $\ln(NINDS)$, α_1, is negative and highly significant. This finding is consistent with the hypothesis that, ceteris paribus, increases in the parent's diversification reduce the productivity of its plants. The coefficients on the other regressors also have the expected signs and are significant. The coefficients on $\ln(NPLANTS)$ and SINGLE both suggest that large firms tend to be more efficient than small firms. This is consistent with the theories and evidence of Demsetz (1973) and Peltzman (1977). For example, the estimate of α_4 implies that single-unit plants are 3.7 percent less efficient than multiunit plants in the same industry.

As we hypothesized above, if we exclude $\ln(NPLANTS)$ from the equation and therefore fail to adequately control for firm size, the coefficient on $\ln(NINDS)$ increases. In fact it becomes positive and significant: The point estimate (t-statistic) of α_1 is 0.007 (4.61). Since diversification and firm size are strongly positively correlated and both appear to influence (with opposite signs) productivity, it is crucial to control for firm size in order to determine the true effect of diversification on TFP.[4]

As expected, the coefficient on AUXSHARE is positive and significant. This is consistent with the view that auxiliary establishment inputs contribute to production establishment output. The positive coefficient on log plant employment is significant but very small, suggesting that there may be very modest economies of scale.

Table 7.1
Descriptive statistics for sample of 17,664 plants

Statistic	RESIDUAL	SINGLE	NPLANTS	NINDS	SAMEIND	AUXSHARE	PLANTEMP
Mean	0	0.07	23	9	0.45	0.07	525
Standard deviation	0.19	—	29	11	0.38	0.14	1,107
Quantiles							
0.05	−0.31	—	1	1	0.03	0	45
0.25	−0.12	—	2	1	0.11	0	144
0.50	−0.01	—	11	5	0.31	0.04	284
0.75	0.10	—	34	13	1	0.10	517
0.95	0.31	—	82	28	1	0.28	4,562
Correlation cofficients[a]							
SINGLE	−0.06						
NPLANTS	0.08	−0.33					
NINDS	0.07	−0.35	0.94				
SAMEIND	−0.06	0.39	−0.81	−0.90			
AUXSHARE	0.06	−0.15	0.28	0.25	−0.25		
PLANTEMP	0.03	−0.05	0.04	0.07	−0.06	−0.01	

a. Log transformation was applied to NPLANTS, NINDS, and PLANTEMP.

Table 7.2
Weighted least-squares regressions of plant productivity residual on plant and parent-firm characteristics

	(1)	(2)	(3)
ln(NINDS)	−0.019		−0.018
	(5.10)		(3.62)
SAMEIND		0.026	0.003
		(3.59)	(0.28)
ln(NPLANTS)	0.023	0.014	0.023
	(7.45)	(7.35)	(7.25)
SINGLE	−0.037	−0.038	−0.038
	(5.43)	(5.51)	(5.39)
AUXSHARE	0.069	0.073	0.069
	(5.67)	(5.94)	(5.67)
log(PLANTEMP)	0.006	0.005	0.006
	(3.90)	(3.68)	(3.91)
Intercept	−0.064	−0.082	−0.066
	(7.30)	(7.40)	(5.54)
R^2	0.0127	0.0120	0.0127

Note: t-statistics are in parentheses.

In the equation in the second column of table 7.2, we replace ln(NINDS) by our alternative indicator of diversification, SAMEIND, the fraction of the parent's plants in the same industry. The coefficient on SAMEIND is positive and highly significant. The implied estimate of π is 1.86 ($=0.026/0.014$). This implies that a unit increase in the number of plants in the same industry raises a plant's productivity almost three times as much as a unit increase in the number of plants in other industries.

The regression in column 3 includes both SAMEIND and log(NINDS) as explanatory variables. Two important observations should be made about these estimates. First, the coefficient on SAMEIND is very small and insignificant, and the coefficients on the other regressors are essentially identical to their counterparts in column 1 (although the standard error on the log(NINDS) coefficient increases by a third). It is not surprising that the SAMEIND and log(NINDS) coefficients are not both significant, given the high inverse correlation (-0.90) between these variables. The fact that log(NINDS) dominates SAMEIND perhaps signifies that plant productivity depends more on the general extent of parent-firm diversification than it does on the fraction of firm activity in the plant's specific line of business.

Second, the coefficients on ln(NINDS) and ln(NPLANTS) are approximately equal in magnitude but opposite in sign. We therefore cannot reject the hypothesis that $\alpha_1 = -\alpha_3$. This finding, along with failure to reject the hypothesis $\alpha_2 = 0$, seems to imply that plant productivity does not depend on NINDS, SAMEIND, and NPLANTS separately but only on the ratio NINDS/NPLANTS. Productivity is inversely related to the number of industries per plant operated by the firm, or positively related to the number of plants per industry. In this sense NINDS/NPLANTS appears to be a sufficient statistic for characterizing the industrial structure of the firm, in terms of its impact on productivity.

Changes in the Extent of Industrial Diversification, January 1985 to November 1989

In this section we test the hypothesis that the extent of U.S. industrial diversification declined significantly during the second half of the 1980s. The 1980s was a period of intense takeover activity. According to un-published Morgan Stanley and Co. data, the aggregate value of mergers and acquisitions increased from $9 billion in 1978 to $57 billion in 1982 to $294 billion in 1988. Bhagat, Shleifer, and Vishny (1990, 56) argue that "many of the hostile takeovers, as well as acquisitions by white knights, aimed to deconglomerate large corporations and to allocate their divisions to related acquirers" via divestiture. They found from case studies of 62 hostile takeover attempts during 1984–86 that 38 percent of the assets acquired were sold off within three years, usually to large firms already operating in the line of business of the acquired unit. Their case studies lead one to expect a decline in average diversification, but they lacked the data to formally test this.

To test if diversification declined, we will use data derived from the January 1985 and November 1989 editions (the earliest and latest available editions) of the Standard Industrial Classification (SIC) File, a subset of the Business Information Compustat II file produced by Standard & Poor's Compustat Services, Inc. The SIC file identifies firms' principal products and services by listing up to 90 SIC codes for each company. The SIC codes are derived by Compustat from Annual Reports to Shareholders and from 10-K reports to the SEC. Our index of diversification will be the same (admittedly crude) one we used in our analysis of the census data: a simple count of the SIC codes reported for the firm.

The top panel of table 7.3 displays mean values of NSIC (the number of SIC codes) and the number of observations in 1985 and 1989. There were 6,505 firms included in the 1985 SIC file, and 7,541 firms in the 1989 file.

Table 7.3
Extent of U.S. industrial diversification, 1985 and 1989

	1985	1989	Change
Mean number of SIC codes[a]			
All companies	5.46	4.70	−0.76
	(0.075)	(0.061)	(0.048)
Continuing companies	5.94	5.67	−0.27
	(0.103)	(0.097)	(0.063)
Births	—	3.70	—
		(0.069)	
Deaths	4.78	—	—
	(0.104)		
Percent of all companies with NSIC in specified range			
$NSIC = 1$	16.5	25.4	8.9
$NSIC \leq 2$	35.4	43.6	8.2
$NSIC \leq 3$	50.3	57.4	7.1
$NSIC > 5$	31.1	26.0	−5.1
$NSIC > 10$	12.3	9.9	−2.4
$NSIC > 20$	3.5	2.2	−1.3
$NSIC > 30$	1.3	0.8	−0.5

Source: Author's calculations based on January 1985 and November 1989 Business Information Compustat II SIC files.
Note: Standard errors of the mean are in parentheses. There were 6,505 companies in 1985 and 7,541 companies in 1989, 3,829 continuing companies, 3,712 births, and 2,676 deaths.

The number of (continuing) firms present in both files (with a common firm identification (CUSIP) number) was 3829. Thus there were 2,676 deaths and 3,712 births between 1985 and 1989. The mean value in 1985 of NSIC for all firms present in that year was 5.46, and the corresponding mean for 1989 was 4.70.[5] Hence the mean declined by 0.76 (about 14 percent), and this decline is statistically highly significant. It is interesting to note that the number of firms in the SIC file increased about 16 percent (from 6,505 to 7,541) between 1985 and 1989, so the total number of divisions (industry-cum-firms) remained almost unchanged (it increased by 2 percent). Over the course of this period, markets replaced hierarchies as the medium of interaction and exchange among a relatively stable number of divisions.[6]

The next three rows of the table indicate that three distinct factors contributed to the decline in the mean value of NSIC. First, the mean value for continuing firms declined; the decline was only about one-third as great as for all firms (-0.27) but was still highly significant. Second, the mean value in 1985 for deaths was substantially higher than the mean value in 1989 for births—4.78 compared to 3.70. Entering firms were much less diversified than exiting firms. Finally, the number of births exceeded the number of deaths.

Since the distributions of companies by NSIC are highly skewed in both years, it may be appropriate to consider changes in the distribution of the logarithm of NSIC rather than in NSIC itself. The mean of $\ln(NSIC)$ also declined about 14 percent from 1985 to 1989, from 1.29 to 1.12.

The bottom panel of table 7.3 provides further evidence of the decline in the extent of diversification. Reported there are percentages of companies in 1985 and 1989 with values of NSIC in selected ranges. The fraction of single-industry companies (those with only one SIC code) increased by 54 percent, from 16.5 to 25.4 percent. The fraction of companies that were highly diversified (e.g., those with values of NSIC in excess of 20) declined by 37 percent, from 3.5 to 2.2 percent.

As shown in the previous section, the cross-sectional correlation between a plant's parent's number of industries (NINDS) and its number of plants (NPLANTS) is positive and very high (0.94). One might therefore expect that the mean value of NPLANTS would have declined, along with the mean value of NSIC, between 1985 and 1989: Firms became smaller as they became less diversified. If so, the decline in diversification might not have increased productivity, since NPLANTS has a positive partial effect on plant productivity. Since we lack time-series data on NPLANTS, we will use an alternative measure of firm size, total firm employment (FIRMEMP) to investigate this possibility. FIRMEMP is available for the subset of firms included in the Compustat Annual Industrial File. We calculated the logarithm of the ratio of the value of FIRMEMP in 1987 (the most recent year for which fairly complete data were available) to its value in 1984 for a sample of 1,562 continuing firms with nonmissing values in both years. The mean value of this variable was positive ($=0.047$) and significantly different from zero ($t = 5.9$).[7] Thus although, as shown above, continuing firms became less diversified (albeit less so than all firms), such firms were apparently not shrinking during roughly the same period. This is consistent with the observation by Bhagat, Shleifer, and Vishny (1990) that divisions that were sold off following takeovers were often acquired by large companies in the same industry. Although this test is not conclusive, it does suggest that the productivity impact of declining diversification was not offset by the impact of declining firm size.

Summary and Conclusions

Previous studies have demonstrated that diversification tends to have a negative impact on financial variables such as profitability, Tobin's q, and (in recent years) stock prices. We have provided evidence consistent with the view that diversification has a negative effect on technical efficiency, namely, on total-factor productivity. The effect of diversification on efficiency might be regarded as an important, if not the main, underlying mechanism by which diversification influences financial variables.

Our analysis, based on Census Bureau data for over 17,000 plants in 1980, indicated that the greater the number of industries in which the parent firm operates, the lower the productivity of its plants, provided the number of the parent firm's plants (and other variables) remains constant. This suggests that the conglomerate merger boom of the late 1960s may have contributed to the slowdown in U.S. productivity growth that began at or slightly after that time.

If diversification is bad for productivity, and therefore for profitability, why did managers pursue aggressive diversification strategies in the late 1960s? One explanation is that managers were interested in maximizing shareholder wealth, but they miscalculated and expected diversifying acquisitions to yield profitable synergies. An alternative explanation is in the spirit of Jensen's free cash-flow theory. Firms were generating large cash flows, their managers preferred using these cash flows to finance acquisitions to paying dividends to shareholders, and the latter were unable to force managers to do so. Due to vigorous antitrust enforcement, managers were unable to acquire firms in the same line of business, which would have been both technically efficient and highly profitable, though not necessarily socially desirable, since such acquisitions might have resulted in higher prices to consumers. Therefore firms acquired business units in unrelated industries, even though they knew little about these businesses and were unlikely to be able to manage them efficiently.[8]

The extent of industrial diversification declined significantly during the second half of the 1980s. The mean number of industries in which firms operated declined by 14 percent from January 1985 to November 1989. Two factors contributed to this decline: Firms that emerged during this period were much less diversified than those that went bankrupt or were liquidated, and surviving firms reduced the number of industries in which they operated. The fraction of companies that were highly diversified, that operated in more than 20 industries, declined 37 percent, and the fraction of single-industry companies increased 54 percent. The apparent acceleration in the rate of decline of industrial diversification from the 1970s to the 1980s contributed to the acceleration in the rate of U.S. productivity growth.[9]

8   Airline Mergers

with Moshe Kim

This chapter extends the research on the consequences of control changes for economic performance by analyzing the effects of mergers on prices, costs, productivity, and capacity utilization in the U.S. air transportation industry during the period 1970–84. The rate of merger and takeover activity in this industry increased sharply in about 1979. There was only one significant merger involving U.S. airlines during the years 1970–78, but four mergers during 1979–81. Although this increase may partly reflect an acceleration in merger and takeover activity throughout the economy at around this time, it is probably largely attributable to the deregulation of the industry that occurred in the late 1970s. These and subsequent developments have stimulated an intense debate about the effects and desirability of airline mergers.

In a recent study Morrison and Winston (1989) evaluated the effect of airline mergers (excluding the Texas Air acquisitions) during 1986–87 on travelers' welfare. They accounted for both price and nonprice effects, using an empirical model of air travelers' preferences. They noted that in principle, although mergers might reduce consumer welfare by reducing competition and thus increasing fares, this loss can be offset by a number of traveler benefits that mergers provide. These include reducing transfer time by eliminating connections that require changing airlines and providing a larger network and consolidated frequent-flier mileage. They concluded that these mergers had mixed effects on travelers' welfare: half reduced it, and (provided that untaxed frequent-flier mileage continues to be provided) half improved it. In the aggregate, though, the mergers had a modest positive effect on travelers' welfare: The welfare gain from increased frequent-flier mileage and cities served slightly exceeded the welfare loss from increased fares.[1] Morrison and Winston (1989) provided evidence concerning the effects of recent mergers on travelers' welfare, but they acknowledged that research is needed to determine whether airline mergers enhance operating efficiency.

Data

The data base that we will use was developed by Caves, Christensen, Tretheway, and Windle (1987); earlier versions of it were analyzed and described in the first three authors' earlier papers (1981, 1984). It includes annual observations on 25 U.S. trunk and local service airlines for 1970–84, and on 10 (start-up) airlines for 1982–84. The underlying source of the data is the Civil Aeronautics Board's Form 41 report filed annually by each air carrier.

For each observation the data base reports the value and quantity of output and of five inputs:[2] labor, fuel, flight equipment, and ground property and equipment; all other inputs are labeled materials. Output and some of the inputs are actually multilateral indexes of a number of components. Output is a multilateral index of revenue passenger-miles (RPM) of scheduled service, RPM of charter service, revenue ton-miles (RTM) of mail, and RTM of all other freight. Since, as Morrison and Winston (1989) have shown, travelers value attributes such as travel and transfer time and schedule delay, this producer output index is a very imperfect index of true input in travelers' utility functions. However, errors in measuring the "quality" of output pose a problem for determining the effects of mergers only to the extent that changes in these errors are correlated with mergers. Morrison and Winston found that frequent-flier mileage was the only component of output quality significantly affected by merger. But apparently frequent-flier miles flown by passengers are generally included in the RPM data reported by airlines.[3] Therefore our output quantity and price indexes capture, or "adjust for," this aspect of output quality. Also frequent-flier programs were much less important during our sample period than they were in the more recent period examined by Morrison and Winston (1989).

Labor is an index of 15 categories of employees, flight equipment is an index of 9 aircraft categories, and materials is an index of 7 categories of materials input. The output and input quantity indexes are all normalized so that their values equal 1.0 for Delta Airlines in 1977.

In addition to these variables, the data base includes three characteristics of airline operations: the number of points served, load factor (the ratio of seat-miles sold to seat-miles actually flown), and average stage length (the average distance between takeoffs and landings). Caves et al (1984) have demonstrated that these characteristics are important determinants of the cost of providing airline services. We calculated the number of seat-miles flown (FLOWN) by dividing the output index by the load factor.

Our objective is to compare the performance of carriers involved in a merger with that of other carriers in the years both before and after the merger occurred and to calculate the difference between the before and after comparisons. The following five mergers occurred during our sample period:

Year	Merger
1972	Northeast merged with Delta
1979	North Central and Southern merged to form Republic
1980	National merged with Pan American
1980	Air West merged with Republic
1981	Texas International merged with Continental

A key feature of our approach is that we added together the values and quantities of output and inputs of two airlines for the years prior to their merger. This enabled us to contrast the relative efficiency of a given bundle of resources under divided ownership and control to its relative efficiency under common ownership. The unit cost or total-factor productivity (TFP) of the pre-merger firm aggregates are essentially weighted averages of the unit costs or TFP of the two component carriers, with weights proportional to the relative sizes (total costs) of the latter.

After adding up the value and quantity data for pre-merger observations, we calculated for all observations a number of additional variables. We calculated the implicit price of output (PQ) and of the five inputs ($P_1, \ldots, P_5$) by computing the ratio of its value to its quantity. We calculated the cost share of each of the five inputs ($S_1, \ldots, S_5$) by calculating the ratio of its value to the sum of the values of all inputs. We constructed Divisia-type indexes of the quantity and price of total input, as follows:

$$QI = \exp\{\Sigma_i(S_i * \ln Q_i)\},$$

$$PI = \exp\{\Sigma_i(S_i * \ln P_i)\},$$

where QI and PI are the quantity and price, respectively, of total input and Q_i is the quantity of input i ($i = 1, \ldots, 5$). We then constructed an index of total-factor productivity by computing the ratio of output quantity Q to input quantity QI. Load factor (LOAD) was defined as the ratio of Q to FLOWN; for the pre-merger observations, LOAD is equivalent to a weighted average of the load factors of the two airlines, with weights based on their respective values of potential output FLOWN. Average stage length (LENGTH) for these observations was defined as a weighted average of the stage lengths of the two airlines, with weights based on their respective values of actual output Q.

Unfortunately, although Douglas Caves et al. (1987) constructed a data base that contains 420 observations, they consider only 272 (65 percent) of the observations to be reliable and meaningful because of missing significant data and strikes exceeding 25 days. We eliminated from the sample the 148 observations identified by them as having bad data. Some of these observations were of airlines about to merge with other airlines. Therefore some of the pre-merger observations in our merger-aggregated data set represent only one of the two carriers that merged. Including these observations in the sample precludes obtaining meaningful estimates of the effect of mergers on the levels of values and quantities, such as total cost and output quantity. However, assuming that the data are randomly missing, we can still obtain unbiased estimates of the effects of mergers on ratios of variables such as prices (ratios of value to quantity), unit cost, TFP, and LOAD. The efficiency of our estimates might be improved by giving less weight to incomplete pre-merger observations based on only one of the two airlines.[4]

Methodology

We seek to measure the effect of mergers on a set of interrelated airline performance variables. To determine the effect on any particular variable X, we will estimate an equation of the form

$$\ln X_{jt} = \pi + \delta_t + \Sigma_{r=1}^{4} \beta_r M_{jt-r} + \Sigma_{s=1}^{4} \alpha_s M_{jt+s} + \varepsilon_{jt}, \tag{1}$$

where X_{jt} is the value of the variable for airline j in year t; π is the intercept; δ_t is a "fixed effect" for year t; M_{jt-r} is a dummy variable equal to one if airline j merged in year $t - r$ ($r = 1, \ldots, 4$), and otherwise equal to zero; M_{jt+s} is similarly defined; and ε is a disturbance term. (We will also generalize the model by replacing the intercept π with a set of airline fixed effects π_j.) The coefficient β_r measures the logarithmic difference in the mean values of X in $t - r$ between airlines that did and did not merge in year t. We will allow for separate coefficients for each of the four years before and after merger, but because the sample is fairly small ($N = 243$) and the mergers relatively infrequent, we do not expect to be able to obtain very precise estimates of the individual β and α parameters. We will focus instead on the average values of the before and after coefficients and on the difference between the two:

$$\beta \equiv (\beta_1 + \beta_2 + \beta_3 + \beta_4)/4,$$

$$\alpha \equiv (\alpha_1 + \alpha_2 + \alpha_3 + \alpha_4)/4,$$

$$\Gamma \equiv \alpha - \beta.$$

The parameter β indicates how the merger or "treatment" group compared with the nonmerger or "control" group in the four years prior to merger, and α indicates how they compared in the four postmerger years. To obtain consistent and efficient estimates of the effect of the merger treatment, we will include airline effects π_j. In the presence of such airline effects, the estimates of β, α, and Γ are based entirely on the within-airline sample moments. Including the π_j is equivalent to using a matched-pairs experimental design, which as Wonnacott and Wonnacott (1972, 172–73) note is desirable on efficiency grounds.

Of the variables we will examine, the one most closely related to consumer welfare is the implicit price of airline services PQ, defined as the ratio of total revenue (TR) to the output quantity index (Q):

$$PQ = TR/Q.$$

PQ can also be represented as the product of the price-cost margin (MARGIN)—the ratio of TR to total cost (TC)—and of unit cost UC, the ratio of TC to Q:

$$PQ = TR/TC * TC/Q = \text{MARGIN} * UC$$

The growth rate of the output price is therefore the sum of the growth rates of the price-cost margin and of unit cost:

$$pq = margin + uc,$$

where lowercase symbols denote growth rates of the corresponding variables. The effect of mergers on the output price, measured by the parameter Γ based on equation (1) with X defined as pq, is therefore the sum of the effects of mergers on *margin* and *uc*. One might conjecture that mergers increase firms' market power, thus raising *margin*, but that they also reduce unit costs. In this case the effect of mergers on output price is indeterminate, a priori, and must be determined empirically.

There are two distinct ways—one external, the other internal, to the firms involved—in which mergers can affect, and could be expected to reduce, unit costs. The first is by influencing the prices paid by the producer for inputs. There may be economies of scale in the supply of some of

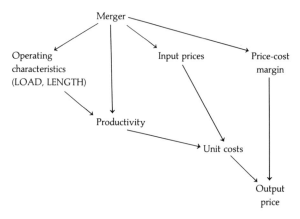

Figure 8.1
Potential channels of influence of merger on output price

the firm's inputs. Also the firm's monopsony power (as well as its monopoly power) may be increased by merger, thus lowering the prices of factors of production.

Second, merger may increase total-factor productivity, the technical efficiency with which resources are deployed. As noted above, Douglas Caves et al. (1987) have documented that two features of airline network operations—the load factor and average stage length—affect output per unit of total input. Merging two airline networks might constitute a means to increase the rate of capacity utilization (load factor) and, more generally, to reconfigure operations in a more efficient manner. Figure 8.1 summarizes the potential channels that we will investigate in determining how mergers affect the price of airline services.

Empirical Results

Estimates of the parameters β, α, and Γ corresponding to different definitions of the variable X are presented in table 8.1. We report total estimates (excluding fixed firm effects) of β and α, and both total and within-airline-estimates (including firm effects) of Γ. The estimates on the first line of the table indicate that the mean output price of airlines involved in mergers was 6.0 percent higher than that of airlines not involved in mergers in the four years prior to merger, and 5.1 percent lower in the four years after merger. The pre- to postmerger change in the merger versus nonmerger difference is therefore -11 percent. The total estimates suggest that merger is associated with a movement from above-average to below-average output price, but none of the parameters are significantly different from zero at conventional levels of significance. However, when we include fixed firm effects in the model, thereby utilizing a matched-pairs design, the estimate of Γ is significant at the 5 percent level, despite the fact that the point estimate declines by more than half. The increase in the price of output of airlines involved in merger is five percentage points lower, from before to after the merger, than the corresponding increase of nonmerger airlines during the same calendar period. The pre- and postmerger periods are centered two and a half years before and after the merger, so this is equivalent to about a one-percentage-point lower average annual rate of growth. Since the provision of frequent-flier miles is incorporated in our output price index, this result is consistent with Morrison and Winston's (1989) finding that mergers increase travelers' welfare, when frequent-flier mileage is accounted for.

As discussed above, in principle, a change in the relative price of output could be due to a change in the price-cost margin, a change in unit costs, or both. The second line of the table indicates that merger is associated with a very small increase in MARGIN, from slightly below average to slightly above average, but the change in MARGIN is far from significant in both the total and within-airline models. The reduction in the relative price of output is completely explained by the reduction in unit costs. Airlines involved in merger had 6.1 percent higher unit costs prior to merger, and 5.4 percent lower unit costs postmerger, than nonmerger airlines in the same calendar year. As in the case of PQ, the total estimates of the parameters β, α, and Γ are not very significant (although highly suggestive), but the within-airline estimate of Γ is significant. It implies that the average annual rate of unit cost growth of carriers undergoing merger is about 1.1 percentage points lower, during the five-year period centered on the merger, than that of carriers not involved in merger.

We now proceed to a decomposition of the effect of merger on unit costs into its two components, the effect on TFP and the effect on input prices. Parameter estimates for the dependent variable ln TFP are reported in line 4 of table 8.1. The estimates closely parallel, with an opposite sign, those for PQ and UC: Airlines involved in mergers had below-average productivity before, and above-average productivity after, the merger. The findings that $\beta < 0$ and that $\Gamma > 0$ are consistent with our results in chapter 3 concerning productivity and changes in ownership of manufacturing plants. There we found that plants changing owners had below-average levels of TFP prior to changing owners and above-average TFP growth rates subsequent to the ownership change. Those estimates of the difference in TFP growth rates were highly statistically significant, whereas our within-airline estimate of Γ is significant at only about the 9 percent level, using a one-tailed test. However, our earlier estimates were based on a panel of about 20,000 manufacturing establishments, while this sample includes only about 30 airlines. Our point estimate of Γ (0.040) is much larger than (about eight times) our point estimate of the effect of ownership change on manufacturing plant productivity. It is very similar, however, to our estimates in chapter 5 of the effects of leveraged buyouts and management buyouts on the five-year (1981–86) productivity growth rates of manufacturing establishments: 0.028 and 0.039, respectively.

The lion's share of merger-related unit cost reductions thus appear to be due to increased productivity. How are these productivity improvements achieved? Two determinants of an airline's TFP are its load factor and average stage length. Lines 5 and 6 of the table examine the effect of mergers on these two variables. Carriers involved in mergers had significantly below-average load factors prior to merging; postmerger, their load factors were no longer below average. The within-airline estimate of the change in LOAD is 4.1 percent and significant. Thus an increase in the rate of capacity utilization is one source of the productivity improvement associated with mergers.

The estimates of the effect of merger on average stage length are more ambiguous. The total estimates suggest that merger is associated with a 20 percent increase in stage length, from average to above-average values of LENGTH, implying that increased stage length is another source of productivity gain. The within-airline estimate implies that stage length declines slightly in connection with mergers. Neither the total nor the within-airline estimate is significant, however.

As we argued in the previous section, declines in unit cost may result from input price reductions as well as from productivity increases. Input prices are the last set of variables whose comovements with merger events we analyze. The last five lines of table 8.1 display the estimates of β, α, and Γ for the five input prices, listed in descending order of the mean cost shares of the inputs.[5] As in the case of the stage length estimates, the total estimate of Γ for the price of labor is positive, whereas the within-airline estimate is negative. But in this case the within-airline estimate (which we have argued is more reliable than the total estimate) is significantly different from zero. It implies that the increase in the average price of labor paid by airlines involved in mergers during the five-year period around the merger date was 4.6 percentage points lower than the increase

Table 8.1
Effects of mergers on selected variables: estimates of parameters based on equation (1)

Variables	Without fixed effects			With fixed effects, change (Γ)
	Before (β)	After (α)	Change (Γ)	
PQ	0.060	−0.051	−0.110	−0.050
	(0.87)	(0.71)	(1.13)	(2.01)
MARGIN	−0.001	0.003	0.004	0.008
	(0.08)	(0.19)	(0.19)	(0.47)
UC	0.061	−0.054	−0.115	−0.058
	(0.93)	(0.77)	(1.22)	(1.96)
TFP	−0.057	0.074	0.131	0.040
	(0.81)	(1.00)	(1.31)	(1.38)
LOAD	−0.044	−0.008	0.036	0.041
	(1.80)	(0.34)	(1.07)	(1.92)
LENGTH	−0.015	0.186	0.200	−0.034
	(0.09)	(1.07)	(0.85)	(0.65)
Input prices				
Labor	−0.003	0.055	0.057	−0.046
	(0.06)	(1.14)	(0.88)	(1.83)
Materials	−0.000	−0.000	0.000	0.000
	(0.59)	(0.14)	(0.31)	(0.06)
Fuel	0.034	0.018	−0.016	−0.014
	(1.65)	(0.84)	(0.53)	(0.49)
Flight equipment	0.018	0.003	−0.015	−0.033
	(0.88)	(0.13)	(0.52)	(1.35)
Ground property	0.000	0.009	0.009	0.014
	(0.01)	(0.57)	(0.41)	(0.64)

Note: t-statistics are in parentheses.

paid by other airlines during the same period. Because the labor measure is an index of 15 categories of employees, two different factors may be contributing to the lower average wage growth of merger-involved airlines. First, mergers may be associated with lower growth in wages within-airline employee categories. Second, they may be associated with reductions in the employment shares of high-wage workers. We found in chapter 4 that reductions in the employment shares of high-wage workers (both central-office personnel and nonproduction workers in production establishments) tend to occur in connection with takeovers and leveraged buyouts of manufacturing firms; it is plausible that these also occur in connection with airline mergers. We also found that control changes have no effect or a small positive effect on the wage rates of production workers, but they have a large negative effect on the wage rates of white-collar employees.

Surveying the remainder of the input price estimates, the only other input price for which the within-airline estimate of Γ is even marginally significant is the price of flight equipment. The estimate implies that mergers are associated with 3.3 percent reductions in the average price of flight equipment over a five-year period.

Conclusions

In this chapter we have analyzed the effect of mergers on various aspects of airline performance during the period 1970–84, using a panel data set constructed by Caves and his associates. Previous studies have examined the impact of airline mergers on fares and other determinants of traveler welfare, but we are not aware of any previous evidence on their impact on airline operating efficiency.

Our estimates, derived from a simple matched-pairs statistical model, indicate that these mergers were associated with reductions in unit cost. During the five-year period centered on the merger, the average annual rate of unit cost growth of carriers undergoing merger was (a statistically significant) 1.1 percentage points lower, than that of carriers not involved in merger. Almost all (86 percent) of this cost reduction appears to have been passed on to consumers: The annual growth rate of total revenue per unit of output was one percentage point lower during this period for carriers involved in merger. This result appears to be consistent with Morrison and Winston's finding that when frequent-flier benefits are accounted for, (more recent) airline mergers have modestly increased traveler welfare.

Part of the reduction in unit costs is attributable to merger-related declines in input prices, particularly the price of labor: The five-year growth in the average wage rate is significantly lower among firms involved in mergers during those years than it is among firms not involved. But an increase in total-factor productivity appears to be responsible for about two-thirds of the unit cost reduction. The level of productivity of carriers involved in merger was below-average prior to merger and above-average subsequent to merger. These findings are consistent with, albeit far less statistically significant than, our earlier estimates concerning the effects of takeovers and leveraged buyouts on manufacturing plant productivity. Our estimates also suggest that increased capacity utilization (load factor) contributes to the productivity improvement associated with mergers.

Our findings are consistent with the hypotheses that the mergers that occurred during our sample period increased productivity and capacity utilization, and that they reduced unit costs, average revenue, and the average wage. Of course one would not expect our parameter estimates to be unbiased estimates of the effects of all proposed mergers. As documented by Morrison and Winston, five out of the nine mergers proposed during the years 1979–82 were either rejected by the Civil Aeronautics Board (one proposed merger) or not consummated (four proposed mergers). Presumably the efficiency gains and price reductions that would have resulted from these mergers would have been smaller in magnitude than (perhaps even opposite in sign from) the corresponding effects of the mergers that were completed.

Nearly 30 airline mergers have occurred in the last decade; many of these occurred in 1985–87. Unfortunately, due to data limitations, the latest merger for which we had postmerger operating data was in 1981. It is not necessarily the case that mergers occurring since 1981 had effects on airline performance similar to those of earlier mergers. One might postulate, for example, that the mergers immediately following deregulation were "inframarginal" transactions and that subsequent mergers had smaller, marginal effects on performance. A recent study by Brueckner, Dyer, and Spiller (1990) of two mergers completed in 1987 (TWA-Ozark and North-west-Republic), however, obtained estimates of the effects of these mergers on average airfares that are consistent with ours. Their estimates implied that these mergers should have reduced fares in the four segment markets served by these airlines' hubs.

Although our investigation does not provide direct evidence on the impact of recent airline mergers, it provides an analytic framework that can be used to evaluate these mergers as well as benchmark estimates for earlier mergers. There may be some difficulty, however, in applying this frame-work to more recent data: Very few firms would qualify for inclusion in the control group because nearly every airline has been involved in merger activity in the past decade.

9   Summary and
       Conclusions

As the pace of corporate ownership change intensified during the 1980s, so did the pitch of the debate about the effects of corporate control transactions on the efficiency and competitiveness of American industry. We have attempted to inform this debate by providing microeconomic evidence concerning the impact of these transactions on productivity and related variables, such as output, employment, wages, and fixed and R&D investment.

Chapters 3 through 8 explored the effects of several distinct types of control changes in several different sectors. The impact of ownership change in general among U.S. manufacturing plants during 1972–81 was examined in chapter 3, and its impact among auxiliary establishments during 1977–82 was examined in chapter 4. Chapter 5 investigated the consequences of a specific, and recently prominent, type of transaction—the leveraged buyout—again using data for manufacturing plants. Chapter 6 reexamined the performance of firms involved in mergers, acquisitions, and leveraged buyouts, using a different performance measure (profitability) and a database that includes information on more recent (post-1987) changes in control of both U.S. and foreign firms. The impact of takeovers and LBOs on the extent of corporate diversification, and the productivity consequences of this, were analyzed in chapter 7. The effects of a different type of transaction—horizontal merger—in air transportation were analyzed in chapter 8.

The findings in these chapters were consistent with the hypothesis that changes in ownership are associated with significant improvements in total-factor productivity, the purest measure of technical efficiency. We showed in chapter 3 that immediately prior to the change, manufacturing plants involved in ownership change were significantly less efficient than other plants in their respective industries. Their mean relative productivity on the eve of the change was −3.7 percent; this figure may be biased toward zero due to errors in measuring ownership change and to threat effects of takeovers. The relative efficiency of changers is virtually monotonically increasing in the seven years following the change. The point estimates indicate that after seven years over two-thirds of the productivity gap has been eliminated. Moreover we cannot reject the hypothesis that the gap has been eliminated entirely, that the previously inefficient changers have caught up to the rest of the industry.

The paths of output and of inputs before and after ownership change are also consistent with the notion that ownership change functions as a mechanism to redeem inefficient plants. The output, employment, capital stock, and materials purchases of changers tends to decline (relative to industry means) at an accelerating rate prior to ownership change and to gradually increase for several years following the change. Although the market share and employment of changers increase after the transition, they do not increase enough to completely offset prior losses; some of those losses are permanent.

The empirical results of chapter 3 suggest that changes in ownership of manufacturing plants during the 1970s tended to involve the replacement of an inefficient owner by an owner characterized by an average level of efficiency. This raises the question, why did an inefficient owner possess the plant in the first place? If one postulates that the original owner was absolutely inefficient, that any plant the individual owned would be inefficient, it is difficult to provide a satisfying answer to this question. However, another possibility is that the original owner was merely relatively inefficient, an inefficient manager of a particular plant but not of plants in general. Suppose that all owners are equally efficient on average but that (1) both owners and plants, and therefore the quality of the matches between them, are heterogeneous, and (2) owners can learn the quality of the match only from experience. The twin assumptions of heterogeneity and imperfect information provide an equilibrium (consistent with optimizing behavior) explanation for both the existence of (initially) inefficient matches (bad luck) and the tendency of ownership change (rematching) to restore efficiency to average levels.

The sample of plants analyzed in chapter 3 was censored in the sense that plants that opened or closed during the period were excluded from the sample. This censoring (particularly of closing plants) may have introduced selection bias into our estimates, but the direction of any such bias is ambiguous. Under one scenario about the relationship between ownership change and plant closing, censoring may render our estimates conservative. In any case it seems quite unlikely that the relationship we observed in chapter 3 between productivity and changes in ownership is largely an artifact of the exclusion of closing plants.

Chapter 4 revealed that the estimates presented in chapter 3 of ownership-change-related productivity gains were actually substantially understated due to their failure to account for inputs employed within auxiliary establishments. Those estimates were predicated on the implicit assumption that ownership change has the same effect on input levels (e.g., employment) in auxiliaries as it does in production establishments. Chapter 4 revealed, however, that there were much sharper net relative employment reductions in auxiliaries changing owners than there were in manufacturing plants changing owners: The effect of ownership change on employment growth was about four times larger (more negative) in auxiliaries. However, we could not reject the hypothesis that ownership change has no effect on the growth of R&D employment in auxiliaries.

We estimated that ownership change is associated, on average, with an 11 percent reduction in the ratio of auxiliary-establishment employment to production-establishment employment, or with the elimination of 7.2 AE jobs per 1,000 PE jobs. These findings are consistent with anecdotal and fragmentary evidence concerning control changes and with statements made by prominent corporate raiders and investment bankers.

When we adjust our previous estimate of ownership-change-related productivity gains to account for this reduction in overhead, our estimate increases by about 75 percent. From another perspective, overhead reduction contributes about 40 percent of the total productivity gain associated with ownership change.

Changes in ownership are also associated with a reduction (of about 4 percent) in the ratio of AE to PE wage rates. This implies that the ratio of AE to PE labor cost declines even more (by 15 percent) than the ratio of AE to PE employment. Moreover, since average wage rates of AE employees are much higher, ownership change is associated with a modest reduction in the extent of earnings inequality.

Chapter 5 examined the effect on productivity of a highly controversial form of control change, leveraged buyouts. LBOs have been performed since at least the 1950s, but for most of the postwar period they tended to be small and relatively infrequent. In 1981 they accounted for under 4 percent of the total value of U.S. mergers and acquisitions. In part due to the establishment of a thick market for high-yield, high-risk (junk) bonds, the LBO came of age during the 1980s. They accounted for almost half of the increase between 1981 and 1986 in the value of assets traded in

M&A, so that in 1986 the share of LBOs in all M&A volume was over one-quarter.

The research design for examining LBOs was similar to that used in chapter 3 for examining all ownership changes, but there were some differences. We extended the data base through 1986, the most recent year for which census data were available; it had previously ended in 1981. Even so, due to the lower incidence of LBOs (compared to all ownership change) and the recency of their surge, reliable estimates of LBO plants' relative TFP could be obtained for only two or three years (instead of 7) following the transaction. The identification of plants involved in LBOs was based on an external (noncensus) list of transactions and may have been subject to greater error than census data on ownership-change codes.

In several aspects our findings on LBOs during the 1981–86 period were similar to, and confirm, the previous findings on ownership changes during 1972–81. Most important is that the relative efficiency of LBO plants is significantly higher in the three years after the buyout than it was at any time before the buyout. The efficiency increase is particularly large in the case of management buyouts. We found LBOs to be associated with significant reductions in the ratio of white-collar to blue-collar employment and wages. The white-collar workers are nonproduction workers in PE, not AE employees. (Data on AE employment were not available for this more recent period, so we could not adjust the LBO-related productivity gain estimates as we did in chapter 4.) There was little evidence to support the hypothesis that LBOs result in sharp reductions in R&D investment.

Our findings on the relationship between LBOs and productivity differed from those on the relationship between garden-variety ownership changes and productivity. In general, unlike plants involved in ownership changes, plants involved in LBOs (particularly MBOs) did not tend to be inefficient prior to the transaction. Indeed the estimates suggest that these plants had above-average productivity in the three years before the buyout, and that the relative efficiency of MBO plants was increasing during these years. This finding is inconsistent with the matching model we used to explain ownership change. Also the magnitude of the post- versus pre-transaction increase in productivity is much greater for LBOs (especially MBOs) than it is for all ownership changes. For the simple average of the mean productivity residuals in the three years before and after the transaction, the increase in relative efficiency is for LBOs almost three times as great and for MBOs over seven times as great compared with that for all ownership changes. This is particularly striking because LBO and MBO plants have much higher (and positive) relative efficiency to begin with, and the tendency of regression toward the mean would cause these plants to have smaller increases in productivity. Instead of merely catching up to average levels of efficiency, buyout plants advance from moderate or high levels of efficiency to very or extremely high efficiency; they become the shining stars of their respective industries.

We wish to make two observations concerning the large increases in productivity associated with buyouts. First, the increases in productivity, hence in mean returns to investors, are accompanied (and offset) by increases in risk, which we have not measured. Indeed we postulate that the increase in risk—increased sensitivity of managers' financial rewards to firm performance—is partly responsible for the increase in productivity. Second, the causal interpretation of the relationship between buyouts and productivity is open to question. The fact that large productivity gains occur after MBOs may indicate that managers who are willing and able to buy out the firm have private knowledge that the firm's performance will improve (due to exogenous factors); the buyout itself does not raise productivity. (The fact that TFP starts to increase three years before MBOs might lead some people to doubt that the change in control is responsible for the postbuyout productivity increase. Presumably, though, the prebuyout productivity increase is largely publicly available information.)

Our aim in chapter 6 was to see whether major findings of previous chapters were confirmed when we analyzed a new and very different data set that included firm-level data on recent (1988–90) transactions of foreign as well as U.S. firms. We found that despite differences in sample period, coverage, level of aggregation, and measure of performance, the empirical results for U.S. firms were quite consistent with our earlier results.

American firms that merge or are acquired tend to be formerly healthy firms whose financial condition has deteriorated. From year $t-5$ to $t-1$, their after-tax rate of return on fixed assets has declined almost 10 percentage points, from slightly above average to significantly below average. Since another firm is willing to acquire these assets, presumably the lapse or decline in performance is perceived by the acquiror to be repairable. Mergers and acquisitions can therefore serve as mechanisms that aid in the firm's recuperation, detering larger societal losses.

Foreign mergers and acquisitions, and U.S. leveraged buyouts, tend not to be preceded by the declines in performance associated with U.S. mergers and acquisitions. The profitability of foreign merger and acquisition targets is not significantly below average immediately before the transaction. If the profitability of these firms has declined at all, it has declined much less than that of U.S. targets. It is not clear to us why the U.S. and foreign premerger performance trajectories differ in this important respect.

Firm-level profitability data on post-1987 leveraged buyouts were consistent with plant-level productivity data on pre-1987 LBOs: The firms that are bought out tend to be above-average performers prior to the transaction. Below-average performers are unlikely LBO targets.

Chapter 7 provided evidence that supported the hypothesis that one reason that the ownership changes and LBOs of the 1970s and 1980s were associated with improvements in productivity was that they contributed to industrial de-diversification, the dismantling of large conglomerate firms. For 25 years after the Second World War there was substantial diversification in U.S. industry that reached a high point during the conglomerate merger wave of the late 1960s. Previous studies have indicated that diversification has a negative impact on profits and shareholder wealth. Our estimates reveal that diversification also tends to depress productivity: The greater the number of industries in which a plant's parent firm operates, the lower will be the productivity of the plant if all other factors remain the same. The sharp decline in U.S. productivity growth that occurred in the late 1960s and early 1970s could be in part attributed to the conglomerate merger wave.

We demonstrated that the extent of U.S. industrial diversification declined sharply during the second half of the 1980s. Data in the Compustat SIC Files indicated that the mean number of industries per firm declined 14 percent, from 5.46 to 4.70, from January 1985 to November 1989, while the number of firms in the files increased by about 16 percent. The proportion of companies that were highly diversified—operating in more than 20 industries—declined 37 percent, and the proportion of single-industry companies increased 54 percent during this period. Two factors contributed to these changes: Companies that emerged during this period were much less diversified than those that ceased to operate, and existing firms reduced the number of industries in which they conducted business.

Our data do not permit us to establish a direct relationship between changes in ownership and changes in diversification, but the active market for corporate control in the 1980s is almost surely responsible for much of the decline in diversification. We showed in chapter 5 that almost half of LBOs are divisional LBOs, which would function to reduce diversification. Moreover LBOs of complete firms tend to be followed by divestitures of divisions unrelated to the firm's core lines of business, partly in order to pay down debt.

In chapter 8 we explored the effects of horizontal mergers on productivity and related variables in the U.S. air transportation industry during 1970–84. One of these mergers occurred in 1972, and the other four in 1979–81, soon after deregulation of the industry. We found that these airline mergers, like the ownership changes and buyouts in manufacturing, were associated with improvements in productivity. The point estimate of relative productivity change (determined by comparing productivity before and after the change, defined as four-year rather than three-year intervals as before) of airlines involved in merger was four percentage points. Since we had longitudinal data for only about 30 airlines rather than thousands of manufacturing plants, the standard error of the estimated change in productivity is much higher than before. Nevertheless, it is still marginally significant ($t = 1.38$). The estimates also suggest that airlines involved in merger were less efficient than average prior to the merger, but the evidence here is quite weak.

Previous research has shown that the load factor (the ratio of seat-miles sold to seat-miles actually flown) is an important determinant of airline productivity. We found that carriers involved in mergers had significantly below-average load factors prior to merger, and essentially average load factors after merger. Thus at least part of the merger-related productivity improvement was attributable to catching up to industry-average rates of capacity utilization.

As a result of their above-average productivity increases, and to a lesser extent their below-average increases in the prices of inputs (particularly labor and flight equipment), carriers involved in mergers had significantly lower increases in unit costs. Their average annual rate of unit cost growth during the five-year period centered on the merger was 1.2 percentage points lower. It appears that almost all of this cost reduction was passed on to consumers: The average annual increase in the implicit price of output (the ratio of total revenue to the index of real output) was 1.0 percentage points lower among airlines involved in mergers.

Notes

Chapter 1

1. As Smith and Walter (1991) observe, an "extraordinary volume of mergers and acquisitions" also took place in Europe in the second half of the 1980s. These transactions will be further discussed and analyzed in chapter 6.

2. The Brady Commission, appointed by President Reagan to determine the causes of the October 1987 stock market crash, concluded that the committee's consideration of this proposal was one of the major factors precipitating the crash. The proposal was not adopted.

3. The magnitude of the takeover premium depends on the market's estimate of the probability that the announced takeover will be completed, as well as on the expected increase in earnings and dividends that will result if it is completed.

4. Malkiel (1990, 104) observes that, in general, "future earnings growth is not easily estimated, even by market professionals." The variance of the forecast error is undoubtedly even larger when there is a change in control.

5. The possibility of downwardly biased estimates due to "threat effects" was originally developed in the literature on the effect of unionization on wages.

6. This file was formerly called the Longitudinal Establishment Database (LED).

7. These are the only events that would result in a plant's exclusion from the sample. If a plant was purchased by a broker, and then resold to another firm or transferred to another industry—a not uncommon event during takeovers of the 1980s—it would remain in the sample.

8. As discussed in chapter 5, the point estimates of survival rates (probabilities of not closing) are slightly higher for buyout plants than for nonbuyout plants, although the differences between the survival rates are not significantly different from zero. Hence our estimates of the relative productivity of buyout plants do not appear to be biased upward by different attrition rates.

9. Hirschman (1970, 3).

Chapter 2

1. In chapter 4 we acknowledge that our estimate of the reduction in R associated with ownership change might be biased because of unmeasured transfers of employees between auxiliaries of the acquired and acquiring firms. We attempt to assess the direction and magnitude of this potential bias in two ways, and find that there is much stronger evidence in support of the contrary position that our estimate is conservative, although the possibility of overstatement of the R reduction cannot be ruled out.

Chapter 3

1. The effects of mergers on stock prices are examined in Hogarty (1970), Weston and Mansinghka (1971), Melicher and Rush (1974), Halpern (1973, 1983), and Jensen and Ruback (1983).

2. Similar ideas are expressed in John Kenneth Galbraith, The New Industrial State (Houghton Mifflin, 1967), and in Robin Marris, The Economic Theory of "Managerial" Capitalism (Free Press of Glencoe, 1964).

3. Gort's model is essentially a variation on the theme of maximizing stockholder wealth. The market expects no gain to result from the merger because the acquiring firms have expectations different from those of the market. The premium earned by the acquired firm is therefore exactly offset by a loss to the acquiring firm's shareholders.

4. See also Altonji and Shakotko (1987). These authors found that the positive correlation between job tenure and earnings is caused by the association between job tenure and an unobservable variable measuring the quality of the match between employee and employer.

5. This implies that firms with an absolute disadvantage are sold because they will have all bad matches.

6. In practice, of course, the quality of the match may be somewhat predictable. We abstract from this by focusing on the unpredictable component of the variation in match quality.

7. For example, each plant is designated as single unit or multiunit, depending on whether its owner operates one or more than one. A change in a plant's status will result in a change in its identification number, although the plant may not have been involved in an ownership change.

8. Since inefficient plants tend to have low rates of employment growth, in controlling for employment, we might have underestimated the effect of productivity on the probability of ownership change if all else is equal.

9. With respect to the second column of table 3.4, we can reject the hypothesis that the point estimates of single and multiple changers are the same at a 5 percent level of significance.

10. The differences are estimates of the parameter β in the following regression model: $Residual_{t+i} = \beta_i OC_t + W_{t+i}$ ($i = -7, -6, \ldots, 6, 7$), where OC_t equals 1 if the plant changed owners between $t - 1$ and t, and 0 otherwise, and the residuals are computed from within-industry production functions.

11. $TFP_t = TFP_t^* + \eta_t$, and $TFP_{t-6} = TFP_{t-6}^* + \eta_{t-6}$, where the asterisk denotes the true unobserved level of TFP and η_t, η_{t-6} are classical disturbance terms: $\Delta TFP = TFP_t - TFP_{t-6} = TFP_t^* - TFP_{t-6}^* + \eta_t - \eta_{t-6} = \Delta TFP^* + \eta_t - \eta_{t-6}$. If we assume that $\eta_t = \eta_{t-6}$ (permanent measurement error), then $\Delta TFP = \Delta TFP^*$.

12. This follows from the classical error-in-variables model.

13. The differences are the parameter estimates of β_i derived from regressions of the following form: $\ln(X_{t+i}/X_{t+i-1}) = \alpha_i + \beta_i OC_t$ ($i = -7, -6, \ldots, 6, 7$), where OC_t equals 1 if the plant changed owners between $t - 1$ and t, 0 otherwise. X refers to the specific variables considered in table 3.7. All of these growth rates were standardized by industry.

14. The abrogation of implicit contracts need not involve layoffs; work rules and other nonpecuniary aspects of labor relations may change instead.

15. Addressing another aspect of sample selection bias, we contend that the overrepresentation of large plants in this sample may cause us to underestimate the improvement in performance associated with ownership change. While combinations of small plants and large firms are rarely challenged on efficiency grounds, the possibility that combinations of large plants and large firms lead to productivity gains is regarded with greater skepticism. Transactions of this type are prominent in this sample.

Chapter 4

1. Wall Street Journal (1989, p. A3).

2. The Economist (1989, 55, 56).

3. Kaplan did not have access to wage data. Two additional studies of the effect of takeovers on employment have appeared since this chapter was completed: Bhagat, Shleifer, and Vishny (1990), and Denis (1991).

4. U.S. Bureau of the Census (1986, A-1, 2).

5. In contrast, according to the Current Population Survey, about 11 percent of all nonfarm employed persons identify themselves as managers and administrators. See U.S. Bureau of Labor Statistics (1980, 34).

6. The National Science Foundation, on the basis of its annual survey of industrial R&D, estimates that there were 510,000 full-time scientists and engineers engaged in R&D in industry in 1982.

7. As discussed below, a substantial fraction of the establishments that were ever observed were observed in only one year, presumably due to closing and opening of establishments. Since 1982 was a very severe recession year, our sample period is probably not representative of the entire recent postwar era.

8. We lack data on nonmanufacturing production establishments, so to contrast the effects of takeovers on auxiliary establishments with their effects on production establishments, we present estimates for auxiliary establishments in manufacturing.

9. Brown and Medoff (1988, 22–23) reported that including in their sample firms that closed did not materially affect their results.

10. Brown and Medoff found that 16 percent of all workers sampled were involved in a change in ownership over a five-year period.

11. The change between 1977 and 1982 in the logarithms of the Consumer Price Index and of the GNP Implicit Price Deflator were 0.466 and 0.390, respectively.

12. We have also calculated the fraction of establishments going from zero R&D employment in 1977 to positive R&D employment in 1982, as well as the fraction going from positive to zero R&D employment. The differences between the ownership-change and no-change fractions were small and insignificant.

13. Data limitations forced us to define t as 1981 rather than 1982.

14. Average payroll per employee in 1982 for PP, NP, and A workers was 16.5, 25.2, and 29.8 thousand dollars, respectively.

15. This analysis will not have implications for our previous measures of labor-input or TFP growth, since these were already based on appropriately, (relative-wage) weighted index of PP and NP.

16. The relative wage (payroll per employee) displays a similar pattern, falling from -0.020 in year $t-5$ to -0.039 in years $t-1$ and t, and then increasing slightly to -0.036.

17. If the span of control S is greater in larger organizations, as some fragmentary evidence has indicated, the proportion of administrators could even be a decreasing function of size.

18. Only 0.4 percent of the entire 3.4 million companies recorded in census data had at least one auxiliary establishment.

19. Since we do not observe all of the firm's production establishments, total employment of NP personnel is estimated (imputed) as total nonauxiliary employment (known) times the ratio $\Sigma NP/\Sigma(NP + PP)$, where the summation is over observed production establishments. This procedure assumes that the employment

share of NP workers in observed establishments is an unbiased estimate of the corresponding share in all establishments.

Chapter 5

1. Economic theory and empirical evidence indicate that the rate of TFP growth also determines a number of key macroeconomic variables such as the growth in per-capita output, the inflation rate, and the real wage (e.g., see Solow 1957).

2. To simplify the calculation of pooled estimates, we made these estimates using data only for plants that were continually observed during the sample period (1972—86); plants that closed or were not continually sampled by the Census Bureau were excluded. This reduced the total number of plants in the sample by 37 percent (from 20,493 to 12,895) but the number of LBO plants by only 11 percent (from 1,101 to 983). The issue of potential bias in the estimates due to the exclusion of closed plants is discussed below.

3. Unlike the median, the mean allows us to take into account (through weighting) the differential reliability (heteroskedasticity) of the observations.

4. If this were the case, it would raise the question of why the plants were sold to public companies.

5. We have evidence that is consistent with the third assumption: the mean 1980 productivity residual of plants that closed in 1981 is -8.6 percent (t value = 6.6).

6. We were unable to obtain similar data for $k < -2$ or $k > 2$. To conserve space, we report here only estimates for all buyouts; estimates for MBOs are available upon request.

7. The growth rate of a ratio, such as E_N/E_P, is equal to the growth rate of the numerator minus the growth rate of the denominator.

8. Hall (1990) also found that companies acquired through LBO did not perform much R&D prior to the transaction. She concluded that LBOs do not have a major direct effect on the determination of R&D investment in the U.S. economy.

9. Including the lagged dependent variable in (5) with a coefficient (π_k) not constrained to equal 1 allows the pre- versus postbuyout change in Z to depend on the prebuyout level of Z, for example, because of the regression toward the mean.

Chapter 6

1. We obtained very similar estimates when the numerator of this ratio was redefined as net income plus interest and related expense. This is not surprising, since, as Carlton and Perloff (1990, 366) observe, "although . . . various measures of

rates of return . . . are different, one is not likely to obtain very different qualitative results by using one measure rather than another . . . . In fact, Liebowitz (1982) has shown that different measures of rates of return tend to be highly correlated."

2. The data item that enables us to determine whether (and, if so, when) a firm has been involved in one of these transactions is the inactive company status marker (and the inactive company status date). Values of 01 and 06 of the status marker denote acquisition or merger and leveraged buyout, respectively.

3. See Smith and Walter (1991) for data on the complete universe of U.S. and foreign mergers during the period 1985–89. They show that the growth during this period in the number and value of foreign transactions was much higher than the corresponding growth in U.S. transactions.

4. We considered standardizing the data by industry, country, and year, but we felt that (especially in the case of foreign firms) the sample was too small to do this for any reasonably disaggregated industry classification scheme.

5. Hirschman (1970, 3). Lapses in performance that are perceived to be irreparable may result in bankruptcy or liquidation. These events are much less common within our sample than merger or acquisition: There were 10 bankruptcies and 3 liquidations, whereas there were 406 mergers and acquisitions. The mean normalized rate of return in year $t - 1$ of firms that went bankrupt or liquidated in year t was -0.298 and -0.247, respectively.

Chapter 7

1. Cited by Bhide (1989, 53).

2. One could argue that the productivity of a plant really depends on its distance from the core managerial competence of the enterprise that manages it. We postulate that the average distance is an increasing function of the extent of diversification. This would be true if managerial competence is at a single location in industry space or, more generally, if the number of sites of managerial competence grows more slowly than the number of industries in which the firm operates.

3. The variance of $RESIDUAL_{ij}$ is $V_{ij} \equiv S_j^2 (1 - X_{ij}'(X_j'X_j)^{-1}X_{ij})$, where S_j is the standard error of the residual for industry j, X_j is the design matrix from equation (3) for industry j, and X_{ij} is the ith row of this matrix (the row corresponding to the ith plant). Since this variance differs both within and between industries, the disturbances of equation (4) are heteroskedastic. We will therefore estimate equation (4) using weighted least squares (WLS), with weights equal to $V_{ij}^{-1/2}$.

4. If $\ln(NINDS)$ is excluded from the model, the coefficient on $\ln(NPLANTS)$ remains positive and significant but declines in magnitude: 0.009 (t-statistic $=$ 7.14).

5. Since the unit of observation is the firm whereas in the previous section it was the plant, one would expect the mean value of $NSIC$ to be lower than the

previously reported mean value of NINDS. Firms with higher values of NINDS tend to have more plants, as is the case here.

6. The distinction between markets and hierarchies was developed by Williamson (1975).

7. We eliminated 331 outliers with absolute values of this variable greater than 1. Including them would have raised the mean to 0.110.

8. Wernerfelt and Montgomery (1988) offer another explanation of why firms may be prompted to diversify, even if diversification reduces the firm's profitability. They argue that firms may have excess capacity of less than perfectly marketable factors and that the marginal returns to these factors declines as the firm diversifies beyond the first industry chosen.

9. The average annual rate of increase of output per hour in manufacturing was 1.7 percent during 1973–82 and 4.3 percent during 1982–89.

Chapter 8

1. Morrison and Winston (1989) observe that their failure to account for changes in choice probabilities and for mode or destination shifts in response to mergers causes them to underestimate the net benefits of mergers. On the other hand, they argue that "mergers have largely foreclosed any opportunity to integrate the air transportation system more effectively, thus undermining deregulation's long-run performance" (1989, 69). This effect, which is unmeasured, would cause net benefits to be overstated.

2. The value of output is total revenue, and the value of each input is its cost.

3. Although carriers are not specifically instructed or required to include frequent-flier miles in RPM in their financial reports, they generally do so, according to Clay Moritz, supervisory systems accountant in the Department of Transportation's Office of Aviation Information Management (telephone conversation, 15 November 1989). The issue of accounting for frequent-flier awards has been considered during the last few years by the American Institute of Certified Public Accountants and by the Air Transport Association.

4. When incomplete pre-merger observations were eliminated from the sample, the estimation results were qualitatively similar but weaker.

5. The mean cost shares are

Labor	0.324
Materials	0.311
Fuel	0.181
Flight equipment	0.149
Ground property	0.034

References

Abbott, Thomas A. 1988. Price dispersion in U.S. manufacturing. Center for Economic Studies Working Paper, U.S. Bureau of the Census.

Abraham, Katharine G., and Henry S. Farber. 1987. Job duration, seniority, and earnings. *American Economic Review* 77 (June): 278–297.

Akerlof, George, and Janet Yellen. 1986. *Efficiency Wage Models of the Labor Market*. Orlando, FL. Academic Press.

Allen, Franklin, Gerald R. Faulhaber, and A. Craig MacKinlay. 1989. Unbalanced growth redux. Unpublished working paper. The Wharton School, University of Pennsylvania, Philadelphia.

Altonji, Joseph G., and Robert A. Shakotko. 1987. Do wages rise with job seniority? *Review of Economic Studies* 54 (July): 437–59.

Amihud, Yakov (ed.). 1989. *Leveraged Management Buyouts: Causes and Consequences*. Homewood, IL: Dow Jones-Irwin.

Auerbach, Alan. 1988. Introduction. In Alan Auerbach (ed.), *Corporate Takeovers: Causes and Consequences*. Chicago: University of Chicago Press, pp. 1–7.

Auerbach, Alan, and David Reishus. 1988. The effects of taxation on the merger decision. In Alan Auerbach (ed.), *Mergers and Acquisitions*. Chicago: University of Chicago Press), pp. 69–85.

Baily, Martin N., and Charles L. Schultze. 1990. The productivity of capital in a period of slower growth. *Brookings Papers on Economic Activity*: 369–406.

Baker, George P., and Karen H. Wruck. 1989. Organizational changes and value creation in leveraged buyouts: The case of the O.M. Scott & Sons Co. *Journal of Financial Economics* 25: 163–190.

Beckmann, Martin J. 1977. Management production functions and the theory of the firm. *Journal of Economic Theory* 14: 1–18.

Bergson, Abram. 1987. Comparative Productivity: The USSR, Eastern Europe, and the West. *American Economic Review* 77 (June): 342–357.

Bhagat, Sanjai, Andrei Shleifer, and Robert W. Vishny. 1990. Hostile takeovers in the 1980s: The return to corporate specialization. *Brookings Papers on Economic Activity*: 1−72.

Bhide, Amar. 1989. The causes and consequences of hostile takeovers. *Journal of Applied Corporate Finance 2* (Summer): 36−59.

Blair, Margaret. 1988. An empirical test of the connection between free cash flow and takeover waves. Unpublished paper. Brookings Institution. December.

Brown, Charles, and James L. Medoff. 1988. The impact of firm acquisitions on labor. In Alan Auerbach (ed.), *Corporate Takeovers: Causes and Consequences*. Chicago: University of Chicago Press, pp. 9−25.

Brueckner, Jan, Nichola Dyer, and Pablo Spiller. 1990. Fare determination in airline hub-and-spoke networks. Paper presented at the National Bureau of Economic Research Summer Institute. Cambridge, MA. July 12.

Carlton, Dennis W., and Jeffrey M. Perloff. 1990. *Modern Industrial Organization*. Glenview, IL: Scott, Foresman.

Caves, Douglas, Laurits Christensen, and Michael Tretheway. 1981. U.S. trunk carriers, 1972−1977: A multilateral comparison of total factor productivity. In Thomas Cowing and Rodney Stevenson (eds.), *Productivity Measurement in Regulated Industries*. New York: Academic Press, pp 47−76.

Caves, Douglas, Laurits Christensen, and Michael Tretheway. 1984. Economies of density versus economies of scale: Why trunk and local service airline costs differ. *Rand Journal of Economics 15*, 4 (Winter): 471−489.

Caves, Douglas, Laurits Christensen, Michael Tretheway, and Robert Windle. 1987. An assessment of the efficiency effects of U.S. airline deregulation via an international comparison. In Elizabeth Bailey (ed.), *Public Regulation: New Perspectives on Institutions and Policies*. Cambridge: MIT Press, pp. 285−320.

Caves, Richard, Michael Porter, and Michael Spence. 1980. *Competition in the Open Economy*. Cambridge: Harvard University Press.

Demsetz, Harold. 1973. Industry structure, market rivalry, and public policy. *Journal of Law and Economics 16*: 1−9.

Denis, Diane. 1991. Evidence on the effects of hostile and friendly tender offers on employment. Unpublished paper. Virginia Polytechnic Institute. April.

Dunne, Timothy, and Mark J. Roberts. 1986. Measuring firm entry, growth, and exit with Census of Manufactures data. Unpublished paper. Pennsylvania State University, University Park.

Dunne, Timothy, Mark J. Roberts, and Larry Samuelson. 1987. The impact of plant failure on employment growth in the U.S. manufacturing sector. Unpublished paper. Pennsylvania State University, University Park.

Dunne, Timothy, Mark J. Roberts, and Larry Samuelson. 1988. The growth and failure of manufacturing plants. Unpublished paper. Pennsylvania State University, University Park. January.

Farber, Henry S. 1988. Comment on Brown and Medoff. In Alan Auerbach (ed.), *Corporate Takeovers: Causes and Consequences*. Chicago: University of Chicago Press, pp. 28–31.

Forbes 1989. Born-again stocks. March 20, pp. 210–211.

Galbraith, John Kenneth. 1967. *The New Industrial State*. Boston: Houghton Mifflin.

Golbe, Devra, and Lawrence J. White. 1988. Mergers and acquisitions in the U.S. economy: An aggregate and historical overview. In Alan J. Auerbach (ed.), *Mergers and Acquisitions*. Chicago: University of Chicago Press/National Bureau of Economic Research, pp. 25–48.

Golbe, Devra, and Lawrence White. 1988. A time-series analysis of mergers and acquisitions in the U. S. economy. In Alan Auerbach (ed.), *Corporate Takeovers: Causes and Consequences*. Chicago: University of Chicago Press, pp. 265–302.

Gort, Michael. 1969. An economic disturbance theory of mergers. *Quarterly Journal of Economics* 83 (November): 624–642.

Griliches, Zvi. 1986. Economic data issues. In Zvi Griliches and Michael D. Intriligator (eds.), *Handbook of Econometrics*. Vol . 3. Amsterdam: North-Holland, pp. 1466–1514.

Hall, Bronwyn H . 1987. The relationship between firm size and firm growth in the US manufacturing sector. *Journal of Industrial Economics* 35: 583–606.

Hall, Bronwyn H. 1988. The effect of takeover activity on corporate research and development. In Alan Auerbach (ed.), *Corporate Takeovers: Causes and Consequences*. Chicago: University of Chicago Press, pp. 69–96.

Hall, Bronwyn H. 1990. The impact of corporate restructuring on industrial research and development. *Brookings papers on microeconomic activity: microeconomics*: 85–124.

Halpern, Paul J. 1973. Empirical Estimates of the amount and distribution of gains to companies in mergers. *Journal of Business* 46 (October): 554–575.

Halpern, Paul J. 1983. Corporate acquisitions: A theory of special cases? A review of event studies applied to acquisitions. *Journal of Finance* 38 (May): 297–317.

Hirschman, Albert O. 1970. *Exit, Voice and Loyalty: Responses to Decline in Firms, Organizations, and States*. Cambridge: Harvard University Press.

Hogarty, Thomas F. 1970. The profitability of corporate mergers. *Journal of Business* 43 (July): 317–327.

Icahn, Carl C. 1989. The case for takeovers. *New York Times*, January 29, sec. 6, p. 34.

Jensen, Michael. 1986. The agency costs of free cash flow: Corporate finance and takeovers. *American Economic Review* 76 (May).

Jensen, Michael C. 1988. The takeover controversy: Analysis and evidence. In John C. Coffee, Jr., Louis Lowenstein, and Susan Rose-Ackerman (eds.), *Knights, Raiders, and Targets: The Impact of the Hostile Takeover*. Oxford: Oxford University Press.

Jensen, Michael C. 1989. Active investors, LBOs, and the privatization of bankruptcy, statement before the House Ways and Means Committee. *Journal of Applied Corporate Finance* 2: 35–44.

Jensen, Michael. 1989. The effect of LBOs and corporate debt on the economy. Unpublished paper. Harvard Business School, Boston.

Jensen, Michael C., and Kevin J. Murphy. 1990. Performance pay and top management incentives. *Journal of Political Economy* 98: 225–264.

Jensen, Michael, and Richard Ruback. 1983. The market for corporate control. *Journal of Financial Economics* 11 (April): 1–53.

Jovanovic, Boyan. 1979. Job matching and the theory of turnover. *Journal of Political Economy* 87, pt. 1 (October): 972–990.

Kaplan, Steven. 1988. Sources of value in management buyouts. Unpublished doctoral thesis. Harvard Business School, Boston. October.

Kaplan, Steven. 1989. The effects of management buyouts on operations and value. *Journal of Financial Economics* 24: 217–254.

Kravis, Henry. 1989. Greed really turns me off. *Fortune*, January 2, pp. 69–71.

Lichtenberg, Frank. 1988. Estimation of the internal adjustment costs model using longitudinal establishment data. *Review of Economics and Statistics* 70 (August): 421–430.

Lichtenberg, Frank. 1990. Issues in measuring industrial R&D. *Research Policy* 19: 157–163.

Lichtenberg, Frank. 1988. The private R&D investment response to federal design and technical competitions. *American Economic Review* 78 (June): 550–559.

Lichtenberg, Frank, and Donald Siegel. 1991. Using linked census R&D-LRD data to analyze the effect of R&D investment on total factor productivity growth. *Economic Inquiry* 29: 203–228.

Liebowitz, Stanley J. 1982. What do census price-cost margins measure? *Journal of Law and Economics* 25: 231–246.

Maddala, G. S. 1979. A note on the form of the production function and productivity. In National Research Council, *Measurement and Interpretation of Productivity*. Washington: National Academy of Sciences, pp. 309–317.

Malkiel, Burton G. 1990. *A Random Walk down Wall Street*. 5th ed. New York: Norton.

Manne, Henry G. 1965. Mergers and the market for corporate control. *Journal of Political Economy* 73 (April): 110–120.

Marris, Robin. 1964. *The Economic Theory of "Managerial" Capitalism*. Glencoe, IL: Free Press.

Marschak, J., and W. J. Andrews. 1944. Random simultaneous equations and the theory of production. *Econometrica* 12: 143–205.

McGuckin, Robert H., and Stephen Andrews. 1988. The performance of lines of business purchased in conglomerate acquisitions. Presented at the American Economic Association meetings in Chicago. December 25–30, 1987.

McGuckin, Robert, Stephen Andrews, and James Monahan. 1987. The efficiency of conglomerate mergers: New evidence from longitudinal research data base. Paper presented at the National Bureau of Economic Research Summer Institute on Productivity. Cambridge, MA.

McGuckin, Robert H., and George Pascoe. 1988. The longitudinal research database: Status and research possibilities. *Survey of Current Business*, November, 30–37.

Meade, J. E. 1968. Is the new industrial state inevitable? *Economic Journal* 78 (June): 372–392.

Melicher, Ronald W., and David F. Rush. 1974. Evidence on the acquisition-related performance of conglomerate firms. *Journal of Finance* 29 (March): 1941–1949.

Mergers and Acquisitions. Various issues.

Morck, Randall, Andrei Shleifer, and Robert Vishny. 1989a. Do managerial objectives drive bad acquisitions? Unpublished paper. March.

Morck, Randall, Andrei Shleifer, and Robert Vishny. 1989b. Alternative mechanisms for corporate control. *American Economic Review* 79: 842–852.

Morrison, Steven, and Clifford Winston. 1989. Enhancing the performance of the deregulated air transportation system. *Brookings Papers on Economic Activity: Microeconomics*: 61–112.

Mueller, Dennis C. 1969. A theory of conglomerate mergers. *Quarterly Journal of Economics* 83 (November): 643–659.

Mueller, Dennis C. 1985. Mergers and market share. *Review of Economics and Statistics* 67 (May): 259–267.

Murphy, Kevin M., and Robert Topel. 1985. Estimation and inference in two-step econometric models. *Journal of Business and Economic Statistics* 3 (October): 370–379.

Neter, John, William Wasserman, and Michael Kutner. 1985. *Applied Linear Statistical Models*. 2d ed. Homewood: Irwin.

Peltzman, Sam. 1977. The gains and losses from industrial concentration. *Journal of Law and Economics* 20: 229–263.

Ravenscraft, David J., and F. M. Scherer. 1986. The profitability of mergers. Unpublished paper.

Ravenscraft, David J., and F. M. Scherer. 1987. *Mergers, Sell-Offs, and Economic Efficiency*. Washington: Brookings Institution.

Ravenscraft, David J., and F. M. Scherer. 1988. Mergers and managerial performance. In John C. Coffee, Jr., et al. (eds.), *Knights, Raiders, and Targets: The Impact of the Hostile Takeover*. Oxford: Oxford University Press.

Roach, Stephen S. 1989. Living with corporate debt. *Journal of Applied Corporate Finance* 2: 19–29.

Roll, Richard. 1986. The hubris hypothesis of corporate takeovers. *Journal of Business* 59 (April): 197–216.

Shleifer, Andrei, and Lawrence H. Summers. 1988. Breach of trust in hostile takeovers. In Alan Auerbach (ed.), *Corporate Takeovers: Causes and Consequences*. Chicago: University of Chicago Press, pp. 33–56.

Shleifer, Andrei, and Robert Vishny. 1988. Value maximization and the acquisition process. *Journal of Economic Perspectives* 2: 7–20.

Smith, Abbie. 1990. Corporate ownership structure and performance: The case of management buyouts. *Journal of Financial Economics* 27 (September): 143–164.

Smith, Roy C., and Ingo Walter. 1991. The first European merger boom has begun. St. Louis: Washington University, Center for the Study of American Business, Formal Publication No. 103, January.

Solow, Robert M. 1957. Technical change and the aggregate production function. *Review of Economics and Statistics* 39 (August): 214–231.

Starbuck, W. H. 1964. Organizational growth and development. In J. G. March (ed.), *Handbook of Organizations*. Chicago: Rand McNally.

The Economist. 1989: A work-out for corporate America. January 7, pp. 55–56.

U.S. Bureau of Labor Statistics. 1980. *Employment and Earnings* 27, 6 (June).

U.S. Bureau of the Census. 1986. *1982 Census of Manufactures, Subject Series MC82-S-1 (Part 1), General Summary*. Washington: Government Printing Office.

U.S. Bureau of the Census. 1986. *1982 Enterprise Statistics, Auxiliary Establishment Report ES82-2*. Washington: Government Printing Office.

U.S. Federal Trade Commission, Bureau of Economics. 1981. *Statistical Report: Annual Line of Business Report, 1975*. September.

U.S. National Science Foundation. 1989. An assessment of the impact of recent leveraged buyouts and other restructurings on industrial research and development expenditures. February 1.

U.S. Bureau of Labor Statistics. 1988. Multifactor productivity measures, 1987. USDL 88-478. September 30.

Wall Street Journal. 1989. RJR, in long-awaited move, to dismiss about 12% of workers at tobacco unit. August 11, A3.

Wernerfelt, Birger, and Cynthia Montgomery. 1988. Tobin's q and the importance of focus in firm performance. *American Economic Review* 78 (March): 246–250

Weston, J. Fred, and Surendra K. Mansinghka. 1971. Tests of the efficiency performance of conglomerate firms. *Journal of Finance* 26 (September): 919–936.

Williamson, Oliver. 1975. *Markets and Hierarchies.* New York: Free Press.

Wonnacott, Thomas, and Ronald Wonnacott. 1972. *Introductory Statistics for Business and Economics.* New York: Wiley.

Zellner, Arnold, Jan Kmenta, and Jacques Drèze. 1966. Specification and estimation of Cobb-Douglas production function models. *Econometrica* 34: 784–795.

Index

DATE DUE			
JAN 23 '95			